JAHANGIR

AND THE
KHAN DYNASTY

JAHANGIR

AND THE
KHAN DYNASTY

Keith Miles

with
Rahmat Khan

PELHAM BOOKS
London

PELHAM BOOKS

Published by the Penguin Group
27 Wrights Lane, London W8 5TZ England
Viking Penguin Inc., 40 West 23rd Street, New York, New York 10010, USA
Penguin Books Australia Ltd, Ringwood, Victoria, Australia
Penguin Books Canada Ltd, 2801 John Street, Markham, Ontario,
Canada L3R 1B4
Penguin Books (NZ) Ltd, 182–190 Wairau Road, Auckland 10, New Zealand

Penguin Books Ltd, Registered Offices: Harmondsworth, Middlesex, England

First published 1988

Printed and bound in Great Britain by
Butler & Tanner Ltd, Frome and London

Typeset in 11/13pt Palatino
by Cambrian Typesetters, Frimley, Camberley, Surrey

A CIP catalogue record for this book is available from the British Library.

ISBN 0 7207 1841 4

PHOTOGRAPHS

The author would like to thank Allsport Photographic for permission to use
the photographs on page 6 (top) and page 8 (bottom) in the second plate
section, and Stephen Line for the photographs on page 3 (bottom), page 4,
page 5 and page 8 (top right) in the same section.

CONTENTS

ACKNOWLEDGEMENTS   xi

INTRODUCTION   1

CRADLE SONG   8

NAWAKILLE   17

WAR STORY   27

KHANS OF PAKISTAN   37

CHAMPIONS   47

NAZ   60

RISING STARS   72

THE NEW ORDER   84

JAHANGIR   98

DEATH AND REBIRTH   113

CONQUEROR OF THE WORLD   128

UNSQUASHABLE   143

LOSING AND WINNING   155

THE HIGHEST BOUNTY   164

INDEX   175

In memory of
Nasrullah and Torsam Khan

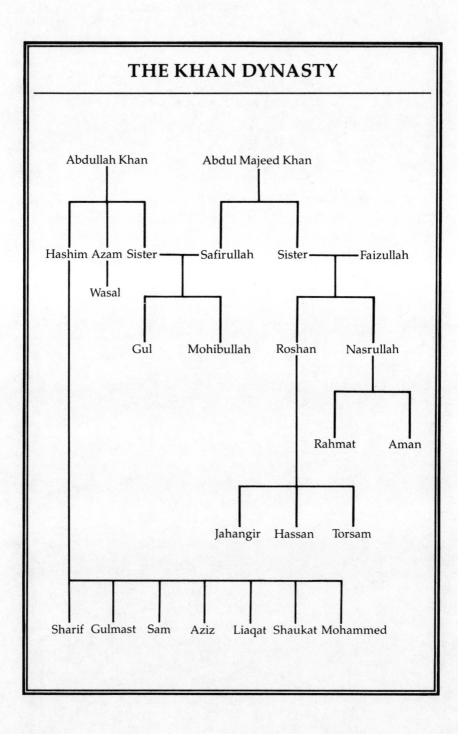

THE KHAN DYNASTY

JAHANGIR KHAN – MAIN CAREER HIGHLIGHTS

1979	Winner	World Amateur Individual Championship
1980	Winner	German Open, Belgian Open, New Zealand Open, British under-23 Open
1981	Winner	World Open, French Open, German Masters, ISPA Championship, World Masters, Asian Individual Championship, Swiss Masters, Pakistan Open
	Runner-up	British Open
1982	Winner	World Open, World Masters, Pakistan Open, ISPA Championship, British Open, French Open, Swiss Masters, Chichester Open
1983	Winner	World Open, World Masters, British Open, French Open, Swiss Masters, Malaysian Open, Pakistan Open, Mennen Cup, Chichester Open
1984	Winner	World Open, World Masters, British Open, French Open, North American Open (hardball), Swiss Masters, Pakistan Open, Mennen Cup
1985	Winner	French Open, British Open, North American Open (hardball), Malaysian Open, US Open, Canadian Open, Swiss Masters, World Open, Mennen Cup, Al Falaj, PIA Masters, Pakistan Open
1986	Winner	Finnish Open, Spanish Open, British Open, Pakistan Open, Canadian Open, Swiss Masters, Al Falaj Open, Pakistan Masters, Mennen Cup
	Runner-up	World Open
1987	Winner	Swedish Open, Finnish Open, Spanish Open, French Open, British Open, Mennen Cup
	Runner-up	New South Wales Open, Pakistan Open, PIA Masters

	Semi-finalist	Hong Kong Open, World Open, US Open, Swiss Masters, Al Falaj Open
1988	Winner	World Open, British Open, Jersey Open, Mennen Cup, French Open
	Runner-up	Spanish Open, Monaco Open

ACKNOWLEDGEMENTS

This book would have been impossible without the full co-operation of the Khan family. They gave me the warmest of welcomes and have been a pleasure to work with at every stage. My thanks must go first to Roshan Khan for his hospitality while I was in Karachi, and for giving me an impromptu squash lesson on court at the Fleet Club. I am also grateful to the naval officer who consoled me in my inevitable defeat: 'It is no disgrace to lose to the great Khan. He was world champion, you know.'

Jahangir's roving lifestyle meant that our conversations tended to be on the hoof. We talked at an airport in the Middle East, during a traffic jam in Pakistan, at a hotel in Paris, at a charity function in Wembley – and that was only in the first week! I have followed him around a succession of squash courts and been hugely entertained. Jahangir's readiness to answer straight questions is much appreciated and his comments on his fellow-players were always illuminating.

Particular thanks must go to Rahmat Khan whose help has been quite invaluable. As well as being my co-author, advisor, interpreter and squash encyclopaedia, he has instructed me patiently in the basics of the Muslim faith. Because the 1987 World Championships were held near my home, Rahmat was able to stay with me throughout their duration. Many of the anecdotes and memories in this book first surfaced over long, leisurely breakfasts or during equally long midnight feasts.

Wives are the unsung heroines of the squash circuit and a special word of thanks must got to Josie Khan. When Rahmat and I were locked in discussion at their gracious home in

Rickmansworth, knee-deep in press cuttings or wading through photographs, food would appear miraculously at just the right moment. Josie was a wonderfully supportive presence during my visits and the couple's delightful children – Natasha, Soraya and Tariq – always brightened the day for us.

Stuart Sharp was in at the beginning of the enterprise. In its own way, his story is just as remarkable as that of the Khans. He abandoned a successful business career to buy some film equipment so that he could accompany Rahmat and Jahangir as they pursued their quest around the globe. The result is a unique visual record, the complete biography of a champion told in six hundred hours of film. Merciless and ever-present, the camera saw the sacrifices as well as the successes, the tears as well as the triumphs. Access to some of this material made my job much easier. Stuart has been enormously helpful and I wish to express my gratitude to him and to his wife, Kathy, for their continued enthusiasm.

Other members of the Khan family made their contribution. Aman, Rahmat's brother, was a wise analyst during the World Championships; Hassan, Jahangir's brother, gave me much assistance during the PIA Masters; and young Amanat, son of Torsam, explained the mysteries of the Pakistan educational system to me.

I must also acknowledge generous help from Hiddy Jahan, Ross Norman, Chris Dittmar, Phil Kenyon, Jansher Khan, Mo Yasin, Sabir Butt and Umar Hayat Khan. Mike Palmer facilitated my attendance at the 1988 French Open. Richard Eaton found time in a hectic schedule at the tournament to chat about his long association with the Khans. Joyce Wadey kindly supplied useful archive material.

Pakistan hospitality was overwhelming and many new friends must be mentioned. Grateful thanks to Achmad Jilani, Monavar Karamat Achmad, Menin Rodrigues, Mohammad Amin Khan, the naval officers at the Fleet Club, the PIA pilots who allowed me to travel from Karachi to Peshawar in the cockpit of their plane, Hanif Khan, Faiz Mohammad, who showed me around the Peshawar Club and then trounced me on the pool table at the Pearl-Continental Hotel, and Atlas Khan, who drove me around Nawakille on his motorbike during the turmoil of an election and who kindly invited me to his home in Peshawar for lunch.

Dozens of books have been consulted. The most useful were *Squash, a History* by Rex Bellamy, *The History of Squash Rackets* by John Horry, the *Complete Book of Squash* by Dick Hawkey, *Guinness Book of Squash* by Michael Palmer, *Squash Rackets: The Khan Game* by Hashim Khan and Richard E. Randall, *Jonah* by Ross Reyburn and Michael Emery, and *The Squash Rackets Association Handbook*. Countless back copies of *Squash World* and *Squash Player International* were pressed into service. *Winning Squash* by Jahangir Khan with Rahmat Khan and Richard Eaton was another important source. Majid Khan's articles in *Dawn* were extremely helpful.

Fascinating background material was found in *The Frontier Scouts* by Charles Chenevix Trench, *The Pathans* by Sir Olaf Caroe, *Leaves from a Viceroy's Notebook* by Lord Curzon and *Plain Tales from the Raj* edited by Charles Allen. Notwithstanding his shameless imperialism, it was good to have an excuse to read Kipling again. *Passage to Peshawar* by Richard Reeves is mandatory for anyone who wishes to understand Pakistan. Constant pleasure was also gained from *The Koran* translated by N. J. Dawood, *An Anthology of Islamic Literature* edited by James Kritzeck, and *The Bible and the Quran and Science* by Maurice Bucaille.

Finally, I must thank Roger Houghton of Pelham Books for the opportunity to write about a game that I have enjoyed playing and watching for thirty years. It has been a labour of love.

Keith Miles

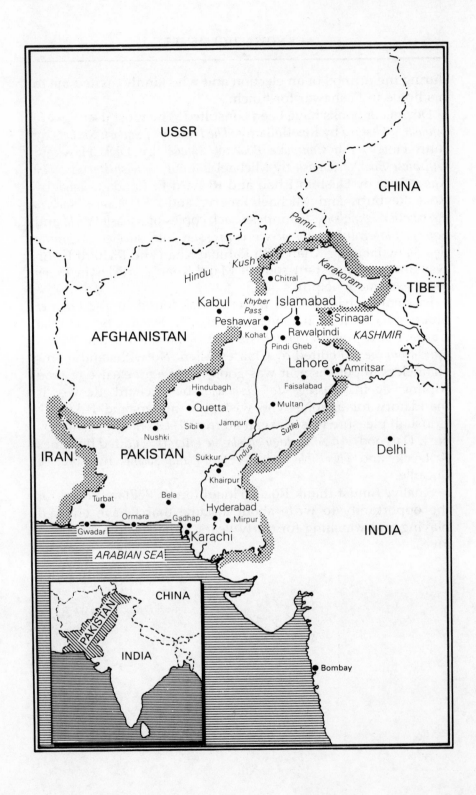

INTRODUCTION

Jahangir Khan has exhausted the superlatives of his admirers. The vocabularies of many languages have been ransacked to find new words to praise him. His rise was meteoric: prodigy, star, genius, phenomenon, legend, with no intervening lapses. He was hailed as a squash marvel. The fittest man on earth. The finest sportsman ever. A symbol of athletic perfection. The ultimate professional. Superstar supreme. King Khan. Master of all he surveyed. The world champion of world champions.

Statistical evidence more than supports these grandiose claims. Jahangir not only dominated the sport, he redefined it. In 1979, he won the World Amateur title at the age of fifteen. Two years later, in Toronto, he became the youngest-ever winner of the World Open Championship. Less than six months after that, he collected his first British Open. In 1984, adapting superbly to the different rules, techniques and court conditions, he became world champion of the American hardball version of squash. Still only twenty, his rule was absolute.

The following year saw another astonishing feat. Six days after securing his fourth consecutive British Open, he retained his North American title in front of a capacity crowd in New York. At the end of the year, he went to Cairo to win his fifth World Open Championship and to lead Pakistan to victory in the World Team event. Fresh tremors went through the squash fraternity in April 1986, when he pocketed another British Open. The unthinkable had happened. Jahangir Khan was visibly improving!

His undefeated run stretched to an incredible five years, seven months and one day. During that period, he played with

1

such devastating authority that only one player – Hiddy Jahan – took him to five games. Those who had the temerity to filch a game from him were severely punished in the next encounter. Those, like Gamal Awad, who boasted that they would bring him down, were themselves ground into submission. During the Patrick International Festival final at Chichester in 1983, the Egyptian pushed himself to the limit in a marathon that lasted two hours and forty-six minutes, the longest match on record. Jahangir was equal to the challenge and won 3–1. A fortnight later, they met again in the final of the British Open at Derby Assembly Rooms. Shattered by his earlier defeat, Awad could only put up a token resistance. He was never the same player after that ordeal in Chichester.

As he scorched his way to sporting immortality, Jahangir left a trail of over five hundred successive victories behind him. He did not just save himself for major tournaments. Everyone could take a crack at him. Week after week, he put his life on the line and came through unscathed. His command was total. He created an enormous psychological barrier for his opponents. All that they could hope for were respectable losing scores against him. If they met J. Khan in the early stages of a tournament, they knew that they would be on their way home the next day. He had a happy knack of simplifying other people's travel arrangements.

It is tempting to say that his fate was sealed on the day that he was named. Jahangir, in Urdu, means 'Conqueror of the World' and that is what he became. But conquest imposes immense responsibilities. It is much easier to build an empire than to maintain it. Wise administration is not enough. There has to be a show of force. So it was with Jahangir. He had to be a one-man army of occupation, stamping out any murmurs of dissent, baton-charging any protest marches, bringing out the big guns to quell armed rebellion. The larger his empire grew, the more difficult it was to police. Defeat at last came. Appropriately, it was in France, a country seasoned in violent overthrow. The date was 11 November 1986. The venue was the Palais des Sport in Toulouse. The occasion was the final of the UAP World Open. The score was 9–5, 9–7, 7–9, 9–1. The victor was Ross Norman of New Zealand.

2

It was the most sensational result in the annals of the game. A golden era had come to an end. Sheer amazement soon gave way to an odd sense of relief. Jahangir Khan was human.

His detractors were delighted. They felt that his defeat was long overdue. In their view, his reign had always been rather suspect. They argued that his pre-eminence was due to the flatness of the surrounding countryside. He had no real competition. Old masters were on their way down. New, thrusting, young talents had not yet matured. He did not even have to beat some players. They succumbed willingly to his reputation.

All this is patently untrue and one of the aims of this book is to prove it. Jahangir earned everything he got with blood, sweat and tears. His achievements were awesome. But it is as well to remember that they did not meet with universal approval. There will always be those whose envy clouds their judgement.

Other critics went so far as to suggest that he was ruining the game. Quite simply, he was too good at it. He robbed the sport of its unpredictability. Whenever he took part in a tournament, the element of surprise vanished. This is a specious argument. Nobody said that Rocky Marciano was ruining heavyweight boxing when he surged on undefeated through almost fifty contests. Did Bjorn Borg damage Wimbledon when he took the men's singles title five times in a row? Should Ed Moses have been banned from competing in the 400 metres hurdles because he was unbeatable for a decade? What of Gordon Richards, the tiny jockey who was head and shoulders above his rivals for a quarter of a century? What of Martina Navratilova with her seventy-four wins in a row and her clean sweep of the major titles? What of Jesse Owens? Jack Nicklaus? Steve Davis?

More to the point, what of Heather McKay, who won the British Women's Open sixteen times in succession and who was untouchable in international competition for eighteen glorious years? Did this bring about a decline in women's squash? Far from it.

Great champions always enhance their sports. They set the standards, raise the tone, add lustre. They inspire. They also gain attention and – in a minority sport like squash – this is vital. Jonah Barrington was the trail-blazer in this respect. A gifted publicist with a fund of good quotes, he brought the game into sharper focus. Hitherto, squash had been largely confined to a few grudging lines in the results section. Barrington won it priceless column inches. He gave it status.

Jahangir Khan has continued the process. At the shop window end of the game, he is the most dazzling exhibit. His career has coincided with a boom. In 1980, the distinctions between professionals and amateurs were officially abolished. The game was truly open. It blossomed as never before. More money, more expertise, more players came flooding in. Tournaments increased rapidly in scale and number. Glass and perspex revolutionised spectator facilities.

Squash was big business. Jahangir was a principal contributor to the boom and at the same time one of its chief beneficiaries. On and off the court, he was a worthy champion. His commitment was ferocious. He dedicated himself completely to the game, tirelessly promoting it and endlessly striving for new levels of excellence. His name stood for high octane performance and his example fired competitors in all sports.

There was much to learn. He was still a schoolboy when he arrived in England and was bound to suffer from culture shock. Because his grasp of the language was uncertain, he was at first shy and reticent. Because he looked so inscrutable, he was called The Sphinx and was accused of being cold, dull and humourless. Nothing could be further from the truth. Jahangir applied himself and confounded his critics. When the full warmth of his personality shone through, he was seen to have intelligence, compassion and a keen sense of fun. In spite of his success, he remained modest and unassuming. He developed into an outstanding ambassador for the game. It was fitting that he was also its first millionaire.

Ross Norman has no doubts about the force of his impact: 'It's impossible to compare players from different eras and say that this one is the best. But I believe that Jahangir Khan is the greatest squash player ever and during his five-year reign, he raised the game of squash thirty per cent.' This is a gracious tribute from another fine professional and it shows the kind of respect that Jahangir has earned from his peers.

4

How did he get to the top and stay there for so long? The most obvious reason is implicit in the title of this book: destiny. Jahangir Khan was not a one-off wonder. He was the latest in a line of champions who had graced the sport with their rich abilities for many years. When his opponents met him on court, they did not just face a sublime player. They were up against tradition.

All of us have a family tree but the Khans have a forest to themselves. Every branch is shaped like a squash racket. The leaves fall in autumn like perfectly executed drop shots. Four factors unite the clan. They are Pathans. They are strict Muslims. They come from a small village on the North-West Frontier. They are winners.

Roshan Khan, father of Jahangir, took the British Open title in 1957 when it denoted the world's number one. Although dogged by injury, he won several other major tournaments in England, America, Canada, Australia and Pakistan. Hashim Khan, a relative by marriage, notched up seven British Opens and lost only once in a final – to Roshan. Azam Khan, younger brother of Hashim, won the title four times in succession. On three of those occasions, the runner-up was his nephew, Mohibullah Khan, who was victorious himself in 1962. The Khans thus completed an unbroken run of thirteen years as world champions.

Even when they relinquished their hold, they exerted a powerful influence on the game. Nasrullah Khan, elder brother of Roshan, was the coach who guided Jonah Barrington to six British Opens, and it was Azam who provided valuable help as a practice partner. Indirectly, the tradition was being kept alive. The Khan magic could still make a crucial difference in the upper reaches of the sport.

A new generation came of age. Sharif Khan, eldest of Hashim's seven sons, was to be the longest-reigning champion of the North American game. Nasrullah's sons, Amanullah and Rehmatullah – better known as Aman and Rahmat – became world class professionals and inherited their father's coaching skills. Torsam Khan, first son of Roshan, was another brilliant player and he got to the verge of the top ten before his tragic death during a tournament in Australia. Dozens of other members of the clan also made their mark in the game. The tide of victory flowed relentlessly on.

Then there was Jahangir.

No other family in squash can even approach this record and no other sport can boast a comparable phenomenon. The Khans of Pakistan are unique and they are justly proud of this fact. Poor and underprivileged, they somehow forged a dynasty that has both adorned the game and enlarged its dimensions. The story of how it all came about is as instructive as it is intriguing. It is an inspiration to anyone who wishes to be a supreme champion in his or her field, and its wider implications have a bearing on the importance of family solidarity.

Any study of the Khan dynasty must touch on four main themes. By its very nature, it is a history of squash over the past half-century or so. It must look at the dying years of British India and the creation of the new state of Pakistan. It must examine the character of the Pathans to see how their warrior instincts were moulded to meet the demands of a racket sport. And it must take account of the special relationship between squash and religion. Followers of Islam embrace their faith as a total way of life. It informs every aspect of their existence. Their game thus takes on spiritual connotations.

Viewed from the outside, the whole saga has the appearance of a fairy tale. It is a rags to riches story with a happy-ever-after ending. It has its share of wicked witches and evil spells and wondrous escapes. It beguiles the listener and reinforces the impression of inevitability. After triumphing over impossible odds, it seems, the Khans were merely fulfilling their destiny.

Probe beneath the surface, however, and it is all rather different. A catalogue of fears, setbacks, disagreements, injuries, illnesses, mistakes, miscalculations and misfortunes comes to light. Luck plays a key role. The long arm of coincidence swings its racket. But for decisions over which he had no control, Hashim Khan might never have competed in a British Open. But for his hasty exit from India, Nasrullah could well have become one more victim of the bloodshed which attended Partition. But for a stray offer from the Navy, Roshan might well have given up the game altogether. But for his readiness to ignore medical advice, Jahangir might never have gone near a squash court.

If it is a fairy tale, then it is shot through with high drama. Unlike other examples of the genre, it has no fairy godmother. The Khans have always had to make their own magic. Dynastic ambition has its own momentum and it can push people along. By the same token, it can crush them unmercifully if they cannot stand the pace. Being a Khan is not an automatic guarantee of success. More than one member of the clan has fallen. The burden of expectation is so heavy that it can disable. Those who have been unable to bear its full weight have been troubled by guilt and feelings of failure.

Jahangir Khan had some additional cargo. In a poor and still relatively young country like Pakistan, sporting heroes take on a special significance: they become emblematic of national aspiration. Jahangir projected the ideal image. Positive, wholesome, indomitable, he brought credit to Pakistan in every way. In 1984, a postage stamp was issued in his honour. It was – literally – the final seal of approval.

Family and country. Jahangir carried his twin burdens lightly. While some players were motivated by the prospect of personal glory or financial gain, he had higher considerations. Winning a tournament had a deeper resonance for him. It was a shared joy to be passed around. Taught by his father, Roshan, coached by his brother, Torsam, then guided by his cousin, Rahmat, he was a true Khan in every sense.

It remains to be seen if he is the culmination of the dynasty or just another stage in its development. His feats will be difficult to equal and perhaps impossible to surpass. But it is hard to believe that a new member of the family will not arise to emulate Jahangir. Champion stock of this quality has the power of regeneration.

The Khan dynasty will go on.

CRADLE SONG

To the uninitiated, all games look strange but squash must seem particularly absurd and futile. In a court that measures 32 feet by 21 feet, two players use their rackets to lash a rubber ball at the front wall, taking care to lift it above the 19 inch tin that runs along the bottom. The object of the exercise is to keep the ball in play and out of reach of your opponent. Only one bounce is allowed before it is hammered at the front wall again. Side walls and back wall may be used as a springboard for the ball.

Danger is ever-present. Two bodies lunge wildly around in a confined space. Flashing rackets can break limbs, smash faces, damage eyesight. Intense demands are made on legs and lungs. Elements of sadism and masochism intrude. The rule of the gladiator is paramount: kill or be killed. There is no visual interest, just four bare walls and a curious scoring system. As a game, it is all squealing rubber and echoing thud and is more akin to punishment than to sport.

Only those who have played squash can understand its rare appeal and only those who have watched the great players can appreciate its full wonder. It is a game of power and subtlety, of thunderous volley and delicate drop shots, of naked violence and soft caress. Positional instinct and tactical flair are important. Psychology can be decisive. Variation of pace, length, spin, angle and trajectory are essential. There is a beauty in the complex geometry of its rallies and a weird harmony in its repetitive sounds. Instead of being a pastime for the demented, it is a game of high-speed chess played out by grand masters on a giant board.

How did it all begin? The question takes us into the realms of conjecture. Certain outline facts are known and some educated guesses may be made but the precise details of how and when squash was born remain obscure. The hand that rocked the cradle forgot to leave its signature. Games with a ball or some equivalent object go back to the dawn of time. Even in a hunting economy, there must have been some moments set aside for play. Primitive as they were, these early games were forms of ritualised aggression. Nothing changes.

The Ancient Egyptians had a game, similar to fives, involving the use of hand and ball. A more sophisticated version of it was found in medieval Europe. Fives was the forerunner of real or royal tennis. This was a favourite game in French monasteries as early as the twelfth century – so the Khans did not invent the link between religion and sport. By the time of Henry V, tennis was established as a game for royalty and the nobility. In the next century, Henry VIII was reputedly the champion of England. He had his own court built and it is still in use today at Hampton Court.

Rackets had replaced the hand as a means of hitting the ball over the net. In 1581, Richard Mulcaster, first Headmaster of Merchant Taylors' School, made this illuminating observation: 'The little hand ball, whether it be of some softer stuff and used by the hand alone, or of some harder, and used with the racket, whether by tennis play with another or against a wall alone, to exercise the body with both hands in every kind of motion, is generally noted to be one of the best exercises and preservations of health.'

This was fives played with a racket, the parent game of squash-rackets. It appears in more discernible form at the start of the nineteenth century when it was played in the walled yards of prisons and taverns in London. The most well-known venue of the new game was the Fleet, which had acquired its notoriety as a debtors' prison that imposed a cruel regime upon its inmates. Dickens gives a vivid description of the place in *Pickwick Papers*. When his eponymous hero is sent to the Fleet, he is accosted by a fellow-prisoner, Mr Smangle, who 'wore no neckerchief, as he had been playing rackets all day'. Perspiration was a main ingredient even then. It is worth noting that the game was played outdoors during a period of enforced idleness, and that rudimentary equipment was used to smash the ball against the high stone walls that hemmed them in. Rackets was a means of relieving frustration as well as of passing the time. Punishing a ball transferred pain.

In the 1820s, the game surfaced at the most unlikely spot: Harrow School. Nobody quite knows how it made the journey from public prison to public school, though imaginations have run riot in the search for an explanation. Emphasis has always been put on the vast gulf between the two institutions. The Fleet contained the detritus of society, Harrow hosted its élite. Yet there are points of contact: both places had a changing population with time on its hands; both kept their charges locked away from the outside world; and both had walls, corners and yards that could easily be used as makeshift courts.

Squash then came on the scene, though its exact date of birth is not recorded. During the 1820s or 1830s someone experimented with a softer, squashier ball that was slower than the hard one used in rackets. The new ball allowed a greater range of shots and easier variations of pace. Squash had arrived but it did not supplant the senior game for many decades. It was seen as an accessory to rackets, a simpler version or a useful introduction. While Harrow boys waited to get on the rackets court, they warmed up with a game of squash against two walls that met at a right angle. They discovered that when the ball was punctured and softer still, they had even more control over it. The rules of rackets obtained. The two games were called 'harder' and 'squash'.

In 1850, two roofless courts were constructed at Harrow for the parent game. Squash had no separate identity as yet. Belated recognition of its potential came in 1864 when a general conversion scheme was undertaken at the school. A covered rackets court was built and four squash courts were installed on the site of one of the 1850 courts. The die was cast. Decisions taken at a British public school were to shape a whole new game.

The example of Harrow was followed elsewhere. Squash was easier to learn and cheaper to play. Courts were smaller, though by no means standardised. As the century wore on, the intrinsic merits of squash became more obvious. It began to emancipate itself: it was no longer a form of mini-rackets but a game in its own right.

Eustace Miles confirmed this fact with the publication in 1901 of a slim volume entitled *The Game of Squash*. It was the first book devoted solely to the sport. Formerly of Marlborough and Cambridge, Miles was a real tennis and rackets champion. He sang the praises of squash and explained how it was enjoyed by thousands of people all over the world. He was keen to promote the game in every way: 'Women can play squash and they should do so. It would make them active and give them exercise (which most of them very sadly need).'

Eustace Miles is important for another reason. He symbolised an attitude that was prevalent throughout the Victorian age – that sport had unlimited moral value. He came to regard it as a panacea for all ills. In 1904, he wrote *Let's Play the Game* or *The Anglo-Saxon Sporting Spirit*. To seduce a friend's wife, he argued, was 'unsportsmanlike'. He insisted that games could give 'a precious elixir of life, almost of perpetual youth'. Headmasters of the great public schools had shared this view. In the same year that those four squash courts were built at Harrow, the doctrine was enshrined in a Royal Commission:

'The cricket and football fields . . . are not merely places of exercise and amusement; they help to form some of the most valuable social qualities and manly virtues.'

This notion of sport grew in strength in parallel with Imperialism itself. Qualities instilled on the field of play could help to subdue hostile enemies in foreign lands. Sport and soldiering went hand in hand. The captain of the team would become the colonel of the regiment. This connection between the playing field and the battlefield was celebrated in Sir Henry Newbolt's famous poem, *Vitai Lampada*. When a British regiment is routed in desert combat, it is the voice of a schoolboy which rallies the ranks: 'Play up! play up! and play the game!'

It was an appealing philosophy at the time and it was at the heart of the educational system. Sport could be equated with war. The idea was accepted by the Army and by the Civil

Service, both recruited exclusively from the public schools. It was these same people who were to be the backbone of the British Empire and who would take the games they had learned at Harrow, Eton, Rugby, Winchester and elsewhere to distant outposts that had become part of the great imperial adventure.

This was how squash came to India.

While the privileged few in England were hitting a soft ball against the walls of their school, momentus events were taking place in the sub-continent. India had always been the jewel in the crown but, in 1848, that jewel acquired a new sparkle. By their conquest of the Sikhs, the British took possession of the pride of the Raj: the Punjab. There was, however, a huge price to pay.

They now had the North-West Frontier. It was an insoluble problem. Geography stood against any attempt at administration: a wild jumble of plains, foothills, snow-capped mountains, alpine pastures and forests. It could be blisteringly hot in summer and piercingly cold in winter. It was barren, uninviting and inhospitable and the sheer size of the area made any effective control impossible.

The major problem was a human one: the Pathans. They were a race of unconquered and unconquerable people with a tradition of fierce independence. A tribal society, they occupied the land between Chitral and Baluchistan and were not prepared to yield an inch of it. By custom and inclination, they were predators. As Muslim fanatics, they fought against rule by Sikh or Christian. And because they were natural democrats, with no man acknowledging another as master, they could not be pegged down by treaties and agreements.

Strategic importance made this the most vital frontier in the British Empire: the Pathans made it the most vulnerable. What further complicated the situation was the fact that the Pathans were not a unified nation. Scattered across thousands of square miles, they lived in tribal groups which were often at odds with each other and which, in some cases, were in a state of continual warfare with their neighbours. They shared a common language, Pushtu, but it was split into a number of dialects. Only when invasion threatened did they speak with one voice.

Imposing law and order on the Pathans was a doomed exercise. The British tried two methods. Their Close Border Policy, pursued until the end of the nineteenth century, consisted in governing the plains and leaving the occupants of the hills to their own devices. When those devices included theft, murder, kidnap and rape among the dwellers of the plains, retribution was sought. A punitive expedition would exact quick and bloody revenge, then withdraw. It was known as Butcher and Bolt.

The second method – the Forward Policy – involved the occupation and administration of the country right up to the Durand Line, the international boundary agreed with Afghanistan in 1893. Such a policy along the whole length of the border was impractical with the resources at their disposal. Besides, if the Pathans were actually tamed and disarmed, the British Army would have to take over the role of policing the border against belligerent Afghans.

Eventually, an ingenious compromise was reached. Pathans were recruited to keep other Pathans in order. No attempt was made to govern or tax the tribes but the Political Agents living among them formed their own private armies, the Frontier Corps. After early difficulties, the experiment proved to be a success. Led by young officers of the Indian Army, the Frontier Scouts undertook highly dangerous work in the cause of law and order. One result was that an extraordinary affinity grew up between officers and men. Once they were on the same side, the British and the Pathans found that they liked each other. 'The great thing about Scouts,' it was said, 'is that once they get to know you, you make such friends'.

Mutual respect developed. Sir Olaf Caroe, who began his career as a soldier on the North-West Frontier and who ended up as the last Governor of the province, had a keen admiration for the tribesmen: 'The stage on which the Pathan lived out his life was at the same time magnificent and harsh – and the Pathan was like his background. Such a contrast was sometimes hard to bear but perhaps it was this that put us in love with it. There was among the Pathans something that called to the

Englishman or the Scotsman – partly that the people looked you straight in the eye, that there was no equivocation and that you couldn't browbeat them even if you wanted to. When we crossed the bridge at Attock we felt we'd come home.'

The Pathans were born fighters. They were proud, fearless and picturesque. There was a swagger about them. They usually wore long bobbed hair and loosely-tied turbans, baggy trousers, a sheepskin pushtoon if it was winter, a bandolier of cartridges slung across their shoulder or around their waist and, invariably, a rifle. Their essential character did not change when that rifle was replaced by a squash racket.

The gateway to northern India was the Khyber Pass, the fabled road that twists tortuously for twenty-six miles through bare and forbidding mountains. Whoever controlled the pass, controlled the route from northern Asia to the sub-continent. The military history of the world may be traced along the Khyber. The armies of Alexander the Great and the mongol hordes of Genghis Khan had come this way but they were no match for the Pathans. Nor were the Aryans, Scythians, Persians, Bactrians, Kushans, Huns, Turks and Mughals. In 1897, the British sent forty thousand men to the area to subdue one tribe, the Afridi. Abandoned picket forts, machine gun nests, bunker hospitals and regimental plaques still litter the road.

Peshawar is the frontier town. It is the great Pathan city, a vibrant, volatile place, more Asian than Indian, colourful, noisy and aromatic, teeming with life and incident, hoary with age and rich in memories that go back over two thousand years. Merchants, migrants, invaders, smugglers, bandits and refugees have all been here. Its streets have been caravan routes from time immemorial and its cobblestones have echoed to the tramp of many armies. Standing at the crossroads between northern Asia and the sub-continent, it is the city of a thousand and one sins with a million and one stories to tell. It is also the cradle of the Khan dynasty.

When the British came to this old city, they built a new one beside it. This Cantonment – or Saddar – contained administrative buildings, military barracks, residences, parks, churches and shops. It is neat, clean and spaciously laid out with avenues of tall trees, broad, tarred roads, large, single-storey houses with expansive lawns, and a bewitching scent of rare shrubs and flowers that always greets the visitor. Time, money and care went into the creation of the Saddar. The new masters expected to be there a long time. They wanted to feel at home. Moving between the old city and the Cantonment was like going from one world to another. The flavoursome atmosphere of a historic town was cheek by jowl with the ordered calm of the Saddar. It was like Billingsgate alongside Cheltenham.

No Cantonment was complete without that distinctive Anglo-Indian institution, the Club, the social centre of every military and civil station. Work on the Peshawar Club began in 1862 with the construction of a red-brick building which still stands. The Club occupied a generous site in leafy surroundings. Library, mess and other buildings were arranged around three sides of a well-tended lawn. The architecture was simple and uneventful apart from a small rash of castellation.

The Club provided the ideal meeting place between the Civil and the Military. All the senior officials would belong – the Collector, his deputy, the Sessions Judge, the District Super-intendant of Police, representatives of the public works department and so on. Ladies also flocked there even though they had no official standing and were not on the list of members. The Club was an oasis where everyone could meet, talk, relax, drink or sit in a cane chair on the verandah and watch the sun go down. Dances were regularly held and occasional amateur dramatics were not unusual.

But one of the principal attractions of the Club was its sporting facilities. There was lawn tennis, rackets, billiards, even swimming in time. The Peshawar Club also went on to establish its own hunt. Fox-hounds were imported from England and the jackal was their quarry. Polo was played outside the precincts of the Club.

Sport was an obsession. Fitness was seen as all-important in a country which had so many exotic diseases on offer. Men and women played and recreation brought the sexes closer together. Tennis was the most popular pastime and additional courts had to be put up to cater for the demand. The Pathans must have thought it strange that so many people showed such enthusiasm for working up a sweat in the hot sun and they watched with amused interest.

In 1901, a major alteration occurred. Roofless, cement-floored squash courts were built on the site of two racket courts. The softer ball had ousted the harder one. Harrow had reached Peshawar.

The seeds were sown. Those courts would transform the game.

NAWAKILLE

The majority of Pathans preferred to live in the hills and mountains which had always been their home. Skill with a rifle and superb horsemanship ensured their freedom and independence. British law could not touch them; they were subject only to tribal discipline. It was the old way and they clung to it. Tribes like the Mahsuds, Yusufzais, Afridis and Waziris continued to offer plenty of action for any British Army patrols.

The Kalil Mohmund tribe, however, came down to live on the plain and accepted the rule of law. Some of them settled in the village of Nawakille, a couple of miles from Peshawar. Nawakille is small, nondescript and primitive. Low houses of baked mud are clustered around tiny yards. Dirt streets are narrow and pitted. Poor people share miserably cramped accommodation and their tiny gardens support a few vegetables and perhaps chickens. Scrawny horses, donkeys and water buffalo do their share of the work. It is very much a male-dominated society where women wear the veil and keep to their homes.

The Pathans of Nawakille did not neglect their code of custom and honour, known as Pukhtunwali. Three main duties were enjoined upon them. First and foremost was Badal – vengeance. They *had* to exact vengeance, whatever the risk, for an insult or injury done to themselves, their family, their clan or their tribe. Badal was modified by a second duty, Nanawati, the Pushtu word for 'coming in'. A Pathan had to extend asylum and protection to anyone who asked for it, even if he was an enemy.

Melmastia is the third element of Pukhtunwali. It stands for hospitality, which must be offered to any who seek it, invited

17

or uninvited, Pathan or foreigner, Muslim or Unbeliever. Hospitality included food, lodging, entertainment and protection often far beyond what the host could afford. The responsibility was a heavy one and taken seriously.

While the hill tribes were still resisting the British presence, the inhabitants of Nawakille were more ready to come to terms with them. There was one big advantage of the Cantonment: it offered employment in a whole range of jobs. Two families in particular were to become involved with the Peshawar Club. They were the descendants of Rehmatullah Khan, the Imam or prayer leader in Peshawar; and those of Muhammad Ali Khan. When the two families later became joined by marriage, the Khan dynasty was forged.

Abdul Majeed Khan, son of Rehmatullah, was born in 1862, the year that the Peshawar Club was built. It could not have been more appropriate as his whole life was to be entwined with the place. Learning and mastering the new games brought in by the British, he rose to be principal marker at the Club and built up such a reputation that his expertise was sought elsewhere. He ran a school for markers and other Clubs would apply to him for these officials.

A photograph taken at the Rawalpindi Club in 1932 shows Abdul Majeed as a short, dark, intense man with a bushy moustache. The calendar says that he is seventy at the time but he looks at least twenty years younger. One thing is certain. By that stage of his career, he was generally accepted as the grandfather of squash and rackets in India. Nobody would mistake him for an Old Harrovian but he was carrying on a tradition begun at the school.

One of his friends at the Peshawar Club was Abdullah Khan, the Chief Steward, a keen tennis player and a competent performer on the squash court. In 1916, his son, Hashim, was born in Nawakille. The boy soon imbibed his father's love of sport and listened eagerly to the tales that were brought back from Peshawar. At the age of eight, he was taken along to the Club for the first time. He climbed the little stone steps at the back of the squash courts and looked down at the game below, at brick walls covered in plaster and already autographed by hundreds of ball marks, a cement floor that deadened the bounce slightly and a roof that was open to the skies, acting as a sun-trap. Hashim Khan was mesmerised.

His story has been told many times but the best account remains his own. In *Squash Racquets: The Khan Game*, he talks directly to the reader in a language that approximates to English without getting too close for comfort. With cheerful candour, Hashim recounts how he got drawn into the game. On one of his visits to the Club, he sat on the back wall of a court with his legs dangling down. The players were fit young men who could hit the ball hard. When one of them misjudged a shot, the ball flew out of the court. British officers were not in the habit of retrieving their mistakes. They simply smiled at Hashim, who jumped down obligingly from the wall to get their ball for them. It happened four or five times.

Next day, the process was repeated and Hashim chased the ball with renewed vigour. The officers were pleased with his help and elected to pay for it. Hashim suddenly found himself with a regular job. After school each day, he would make the fifteen-minute journey to the Club and attend to his duties. As a reward for his services, he was given five rupees a month. He felt he was rich. It was his first professional engagement in squash.

Late in the afternoon when the officers went off to have a shower before dinner, Hashim and the other ballboys had the chance to play on court themselves. Being small, Hashim encountered difficulty with the big racket and had to hold it well up the handle. But he had two natural attributes – a quick eye and a strong pair of legs. No matter where the ball went, he could always get to it in time to play a stroke. He developed his talents whenever he could, both on the squash and tennis courts. When rain drove him indoors, he was allowed to watch the officers in the billiard room.

Disaster struck his family a couple of years later. His father was killed in a road accident. They were on their way to a steeplechase near Peshawar and Abdullah was in charge of the tea party, travelling in a truck with all the food and flowers. The driver made a fatal error and crashed into a stone wall, hurling Abdullah from his seat to be crushed between vehicle and wall. It all happened in seconds and Hashim, also in the truck, was a witness. The widow received a small pension from the Club and had to bring up her four children on it – Hashim, two sisters and baby Azam.

This was in 1927. The same year saw the birth of another future squash champion: Roshan Khan. His brother, Nasrullah, was some seven years older. Four names that were to remould the sport: Hashim, Azam, Roshan, Nasrullah. The Raj quartet.

Those early years were a struggle for all of them. They came from poor families and lived in modest homes in Nawakille. Nobody at that time could possibly have foreseen the cumulative impact they would have on squash. It was still the game of the élite, the former public schoolboys at the Peshawar Club. The thought that it would be the making of some disadvantaged and democratic Pathans was ludicrous.

Hashim Khan, meanwhile, was restive, the death of his father having effectively robbed him of his childhood. He was a boy no more but all he could think about was squash and he wanted to leave school so that he could play it more and more. His mother was strongly opposed to the idea and so he remained, albeit reluctantly, at school. But his mind was never on his work. His first love was a game with a racket and a soft ball.

Following the dictates of his heart, he left school and tried to assure his anxious mother that it was all for the best. His religious studies continued, however, and he went to the mosque in Peshawar every day. It was not his only port of call in the city. He always went to the Club as well, his second home.

Shocked by the death of his close friend, Abdul Majeed was determined to do all he could to help the stricken family. Hashim reaped the main benefit. Through the old man, he now had contact with one of the great sporting families of India. Abdul Majeed had been rackets professional at the Peshawar Club for over forty years, having started there as a ball boy. His eldest son, Ismatullah, was marker to the Viceroy. Safirullah, another son, closer to Hashim's own age, was also an aspiring young squash player. He was later to formalise his friend's ties with the family by marrying Hashim's sister.

Since the old man was usually too busy with his duties,

Hashim looked elsewhere for help. Ismatullah soon returned home to act as his father's assistant. Hashim begged him for some basic coaching on the squash court and, Ismatullah being a good teacher, the pupil improved fast. As time passed, his fitness and stamina developed. He eventually reached the stage where he could press Ismatullah so hard that he had to fight for every point. The coach was years older and had far more experience but these advantages did not hold Hashim at bay for long. The British officers were very impressed with the teenage prodigy and paid him the compliment of asking him for a game. He was seen as a worthy opponent who could stretch them. Hashim had now been promoted from the ranks: the ball boy was now a squash player.

The standard among the officers was high. Schooled in the game back in England, they played it regularly and with a competitive edge. But Hashim could handle the best of them. His speed about the court was bewildering and there was almost no shot that he could not retrieve. His control of the ball was uncanny.

Out of deference to his opponents, and because he deemed it wise, he did not enforce his superiority. Instead, he eased off to make games look closer than they really were: 'This way they think that maybe next time, they beat me. This is good. If you beat a man bad, you keep him without a score, then he has no hope, never wants to go in court with you again. This makes me feel sorry. It is not good sport.'

No tournament professional of today would agree. He or she is out to win every game as emphatically as possible. Sympathy for a weaker opponent is itself a sign of weakness. Hashim, of course, was only speaking of friendly games but something of the same attitude lingered throughout his career. He was more than once accused of letting a match go to five games when he could easily have settled it in three. There were cynics who believed that some of his lengthy battles with his brother, Azam, had a manufactured feel about them.

While Hashim was being taken under the wing of one of the leading squash families, the other was flourishing with equal vigour. Said Ali, the talented son of Muhammad Ali, was a well-known rackets and squash professional, renowned for his fitness. Like his father, who reached the age of ninety-five, he was made of durable material. As late as 1944, he was competing in the All India Professional Championship with a sprightliness that made a mockery of his sixty years. Even at eighty, Said Ali would be seen flitting about a squash court with his long white beard and face of crumpled parchment.

In those inter-war years, however, he concentrated on doing his job and passing on his skills to his sons. One of them, Abdul Bari, became squash champion of India and went on – after Partition – to be the first Pakistani to take up an appointment in England as a club professional. Sadly, his new career was short-lived. He died in 1954 at the age of thirty-three.

Another grandson of Muhammad Ali was Faizullah, son of Aziz. Faizullah coached tennis and squash in various parts of India. In the 1920s, he was attached to the Peshawar Club. He married one of Abdul Majeed's daughters, thus bonding the two families together. Faizullah was a tall, wiry, powerful man with a stern countenance, gimlet eyes and a dark moustache. His pointed turban gave him extra height and preserved a hint of the tribal warrior.

The life of a professional was onerous but not well-paid. Faizullah would be mixing with the officer class in the lush surroundings of the Club before going back to his humble dwelling in Nawakille. He shuttled between the two extremes with calm unconcern. Like other members of his family, his priority was to instil a love of racket sports into his sons. Two of those sons were supremely gifted: Nasrullah and Roshan.

If they were born with rackets in their hands, they certainly did not have silver spoons in their mouths. Nawakille gave them a childhood of barefoot simplicity. The family house was small, dark and stone-floored without electricity or running water. Two rooms with only the most basic furniture had to serve Faizullah, his wife and their six children. The bathroom was a tiny cubicle with a few jugs and bowls in it. Water was drawn from a nearby well. The latrine was of the most elementary design.

Privacy was out of the question. It was communal living of a kind that the Pathans had always known. Beyond the immediate family was the extended family of uncles, aunts, nephews, nieces, cousins, second cousins, third cousins and so on. Beyond that was the clan and beyond that Nawakille, a village of some thousand or more inhabitants, centred very much in itself and perpetuating time-honoured traditions, carrying on an almost feudal existence in the twentieth century.

Winter was an ordeal with a biting wind that swept across the whole province. In the Peshawar Club, the five separate fireplaces in the dining room bear testimony to the intense cold that had to be defeated. The houses in Nawakille did not run to such luxuries. The Pathans relied on sheepskin coats, extra bedding and their own hardy natures to survive the winter.

Summer could be even more oppressive. The heat of the midday sun was so punishing at times that Faizullah and his family used to retreat to a crude cellar hacked out of the bare earth. In this gloomy dug-out, as many as a dozen people would crowd together, curled up on wooden cots. At night, if the house was too clammy, they would sleep outside in the open air.

There were other problems. Disease was rife. Conditions were unhygienic and the water far from pure. Medical facilities were very limited. Mosquitoes were feared because of the danger of malaria but there were several other troublesome insects. Some would bite, others would sting, others would give off a foul odour if squashed. Huge spiders could haunt latrines; snakes, rodents and other wild animals were an occasional threat. Nawakille offered more than its share of gratuitous pain.

Food was simple: chappatis, rice, wheat ground on stones, hot curry, vegetables, fruit in season. It was an unvarying diet and it contrasted sharply with the haute cuisine at the Peshawar Club. The British did not belong to the 'When in Rome do as the Romans do' school of thought. If they colonised another country, they took their own along with them. The dining habits of the upper middle classes were thus transplanted to the North-West Frontier along with the Pax Britannica and the game of squash.

What must the denizens of Nawakille have thought when they heard that oysters on ice from the Peshawar Club, wrapped in a Lilo, had been dropped by plane on an isolated

Army post by way of a Christmas present? Only the British would put food before firepower.

This was the world in which Nasrullah, Roshan and their siblings grew up. It was a busy, bustling, boisterous world, full of sounds and smells that soon became familiar. Because they were close to the realities of birth and death, life in the village had a startling immediacy for them. Like all the other children, they had simple needs and low expectations. From an early age, they learned the precepts of the Muslim faith. They were taught that all men were equal, if they performed – as true believers – the five duties of their religion.

They had to make a daily declaration in Arabic: 'La ilaha illulahu Muhammadur rasul-Allah' (There is no god but God and Muhammad is His messenger'). They had to fast during the holy month of Ramadan. Once in a lifetime, if at all possible, they had to make Hadj, a pilgrimage to Mecca, birthplace of Muhammad. They had to give alms generously and, most important of all, they had to pray five times a day and say Friday noon prayers in a mosque. Islam means surrender to God: unconditional surrender.

For a Muslim, the pages of the Koran hold all the answers. The book is both a stunning example of prophetic writing and a true literary masterpiece. Accepted as the infallible word of Allah as revealed to Muhammad by the Angel Gabriel over fourteen hundred years ago, the Koran gives the Muslim a complete framework for his life. The Exordium sets the tone and reveals the scope of what is to follow.

IN THE NAME OF ALLAH
THE COMPASSIONATE
THE MERCIFUL
Praise be to Allah, Lord of the Creation,
The Compassionate, the Merciful,
King of Judgement-day!
You alone we worship, and to You alone
we pray for help.
Guide us to the straight path
The path of those whom You have favoured,
Not of those who have incurred Your wrath,
Nor of those who have gone astray.

Islam grew up on the sub-continent as an alternative to the caste system of Hinduism. There was an egalitarianism about the Muslim religion which appealed to such instinctive demo- crats as the Pathans. Islam was different. It had no priesthood, no rigid hierarchy, no social pre-requisites and it encouraged initiative and independence in the believer. Devotion was his individual responsibility. Worship was not restricted to a holy place: the faithful could pray anywhere – on a mountain as well as in a mosque.

Self-discipline was fundamental. Nasrullah and Roshan had this drummed into them. It was a valuable lesson. Their capacity for self-discipline would later help enormously in their careers as squash players. Something else was inculcated: they learned to honour their parents and respect their elders. It was not a feature of every society. When Roshan first came to Britain in the 1950s, he was appalled by the lack of respect shown by the young. Because Nasrullah was seven years older than him, Roshan gave him automatic respect and this, too, was reflected in their professional life. It enabled Nasrullah to coach his younger brother in the knowledge that his advice would be heeded and obeyed. Hashim was in a similar position with regard to Azam. Respect due to a senior sibling was a factor in their coaching relationship as well.

Nawakille, then, was an Islamic village. Above the endless chatter, the noisy bartering, the clip-clop of horses, the stealthy slap of camels, the bellows of bullocks, the barking of dogs and the happy clamour of children at play, would rise the wail of the muezzin, calling the faithful to prayer. The cry from the minarets was an ever-present reminder of the power of religion in that devout corner of the North-West Frontier.

The childhood of the young Khans had its dangers. In 1930, trouble spilled down from the hills like molten lava. Peshawar was shaken to its foundations by riots. Instead of being able to play squash at the Club, the British officers found themselves caught up in a much more deadly game.

Complacency had set in on the Frontier. With their planes, light armour, improved mountain artillery and higher scale of light machine-guns, the British Army held the whip-hand over the Pathans in the hills. The tribes were reduced to long-range sniping. It was felt that their teeth had been drawn. The Pathans demonstrated that they could still bite with vicious effect.

The problem began in the prosperous districts of Peshawar, Nowshera and Kohat. An organisation called the Frontier Youth League was formed in 1929. It adopted a type of political uniform then fashionable, and became known as Redshirts. Claiming to be dedicated to social and religious improvement, it was a highly seditious group that tried to set up a parallel administration. Its leaders were Abdul Ghaffar Khan and his brother, Dr Khan Sahib, formerly a Medical Officer of the Guides.

In 1930, the Redshirts were behind the savage rioting in Peshawar city, during which an armoured car and its occupants were incinerated. The Afridis and the Mamunds took advantage of the situation to come down to the outskirts of Peshawar, invade the Government Supply Depot and mine roads. The whole area was witness to violence, brutality and bloodshed and casualties on both sides were high. It took 47,000 troops to quell this attempt to found a separate Pathan state. The Redshirts were beaten but it was a Pyrrhic victory. Once again, the Frontier had lived up to its reputation.

Hashim, Azam, Nasrullah, and Roshan did not appreciate the full implications of what had happened. They were either too young or too distanced from it. But they felt the effect of the riots and heard the daily discussions in Nawakille. Abdul Majeed and Faizullah Khan were closer to the events. From the horror stories that circulated at the Club, they gained a rather gruesome insight into the outrages that had occurred. Peshawar, hitherto a peaceful city with a cantonment that went harmlessly about its business, had been turned into a battleground. British might had been challenged.

It was a learning experience for all concerned. The Redshirts withdrew to lick their wounds and the tribesmen retreated to the safety of the hills. The British Army maintained a much higher profile. Complacency had gone now as the Pathans had proved they were still to be feared and watched. In the 1930s, British vigilance did not slacken again. Army patrols were on constant alert for further signs of rebellion. But they were looking in the wrong direction. The revolution would come in their military base – on the squash courts at the Peshawar Club.

WAR STORY

An uneasy peace hovered over the Frontier in the early 1930s. The Redshirts campaigned hard in the settled areas and they thrived on the frustration of being denied the limited self-government which other provinces in India enjoyed. The hill tribes, too, were fomenting. In 1935 there was trouble among the Bajaur and Mohmand tribes north of Peshawar. Two operations, involving four brigade groups, had to be launched against them. The most notable event of the hostilities was a surprise defeat inflicted by the Mohmands at Wucha Jawar on one of the best Frontier battalions, the Guides (5/12 Frontier Force Regt) who, in two hours, lost three-quarters of the company-and-a-half engaged. Even against superior manpower and weaponry, the Pathans were still a fearsome enemy.

During these years, Hashim was honing his skills on the squash courts at the Peshawar Club. When Azam was old enough, he was taken along and shown the games that his elder brother had mastered. Hashim had fallen in love with squash. He was a little put out, therefore, when Azam showed an early preference for tennis. In time, however, Hashim won him around to the game that would make them both famous.

Nasrullah was now working at the Club as a tennis ball boy. There were twenty-five grass courts, and they were all in regular use, so Nasrullah was kept busy. Like Hashim, he learned by watching the officers play and then practised on his own when nobody else was about. He liked tennis and squash but showed particular promise as a rackets player. It was not to be developed yet. He was only a menial, a ball boy who was not supposed to use the facilities at all. Indians were not permitted to join the Club, nor were Anglo-Indians.

27

It was paradoxical. The British would employ Indians to coach them in their racket sports and yet denied them membership of their clubs. Controversy raged over the issue throughout the sub-continent and it was usually seen in terms of a colour-bar. Some cities had mixed clubs but many places remained exclusive and thus an on-going source of resentment. The young Khans did not worry about this situation but accepted it for what it was and contrived to work within it.

The infant Roshan soon paid his first visit to the Club where his father coached. He marvelled at the tennis courts. He was duly impressed with rackets, a game he would refer to thereafter as 'racket-racket'. Then he was taken to see the squash courts.

Their doors were made of iron and they clanged shut like doors on prison cells. The walls were disfigured by the daily pounding they had taken. Ants climbed vertically while other insects risked the perilous journey across the cement floor. The sun hit the back walls with blinding effect but left one quadrant of the courts in deep shadow. Roshan was mesmerised as he watched two officers flay the life out of a rubber ball. He had no idea of the significance of his visit. It never occurred to him that he would one day beat the whole world at this curious game.

Hashim, Azam, Nasrullah, Roshan: the seeds of revolution were planted. But the climate was not conducive to rapid growth. It would be a long time before the plant came out in full flower.

In 1935, Faizullah Khan was offered the job as coach at the Rawalpindi Club. He and his family left Nawakille and headed for the Punjab. Hashim and Azam stayed in Peshawar. The elder brother was now an established fixture at the Club and made a little money by stringing rackets with new gut or acting as a playing partner on the courts. Hashim took care not to coach or even to give casual advice. The Club already had enough professionals and he was not allowed to trespass on their domain. He was content, therefore, to bide his time. He had no urge to leave home in search of a job elsewhere. His requirements were few: 'I do not need money for smoking or drinking, I am a Muslim, and also a single man.'

Life on the Frontier became more and more troubled. There

was sporadic warfare in the hills throughout the remainder of the decade and lurid tales of Pathan atrocities would spread around the Club. Under the inspired leadership of Abdul Ghaffar Khan, the Redshirts – or Servants of God, as they styled themselves – increased their strength and influence all the time. In 1937 the North-West Frontier Province attained full provincial self-government, including responsibility for law and order. Dismay was caused among the British when Dr Khan Sahib, the brother of the Redshirt leader, was appointed Chief Minister. He had no jurisdiction over the trans-Frontier tribes and did not interfere with their administration, but the sight of a Pathan giving orders to British District Officers was an unsettling one.

These events may seem rather remote from the squash courts at the Peshawar Club but they helped to create the political climate in which Hashim and Azam grew up. Abdul Ghaffar Khan was a potent force and could not be ignored. He was no mere firebrand: with his band of supporters, he was trying to educate his largely illiterate people. His aim was to drag the Pathans out of tribalism and transform them into nationalists committed to the ideal of an independent Pathan State. A man of unshakable convictions, he was to be a thorn in the flesh of the British until their eventual withdrawal.

Nasrullah and Roshan moved away from the area in body but not in mind. Nawakille would always be their spiritual home. No matter how long they stayed away, the village would welcome them as its own on their return. For the time being, however, they travelled to the Punjab. The Land of Five Rivers was the granary of India, a fertile region with grainfields of wheat, barley, rice and maize in abundance. Fields of cotton, sugarcane and bananas could also be seen. This richly-endowed province was in every way more hospitable to the newcomer than the Frontier.

Rawalpindi itself lay on the Grand Trunk Road between Peshawar and Lahore. An important transit point, it formed part of the ancient Silk Trade Route. In the 1930s it was still a thriving commercial and trading centre. Camels and bullock-carts brought their goods to market along roads that had changed little since Kipling's day.

As in Peshawar, there was the same sharp contrast between the exotic, characterful Old City and the British town that was built next to it. When visitors entered the wooded and shady Mall with its air of genteel tranquillity, they left behind the hustle and the babble and the vivid colour of old Rawalpindi. Situated on the north bank of the River Leh, the city was some 175 kilometres south-east of Peshawar. To Nasrullah and Roshan at first, the distance between the two places must have seemed vastly bigger.

Faizullah Khan took up his duties at the Rawalpindi Club and his sons showed the keenest interest in the facilities. Having watched so many officers enjoying the racket games, they could not wait for an opportunity to play themselves. There were two obstacles to surmount: they had no equipment and they were not permitted to use the courts. Roshan recalls how they coped: 'We find broken rackets that officers throw away. We mend them. We play when nobody look. We play squash and racket-racket. Sometimes Daddy catch us and he beat us. But that not stop us. When we get another chance, we play a game together.'

At Rawalpindi, too, the courts were roofless. Nasrullah and Roshan would play with bare feet on the cement floor, twisting and turning, stopping and sliding until their soles were sore. While the officers would have a game in shorts and singlets, the brothers wore only a shalwar, the long knee-length shirt that was part of their tribal costume. Seven years older, Nasrullah always had too much guile and experience for his brother, but Roshan improved steadily. This was the start of the coach-player relationship that would open up all kinds of possibilities for them.

Roshan was only eight when they moved to their new home and he was soon to find a job of his own at the Club. He became a ball boy for tennis and worked long hours: 'Maybe six, maybe seven hours a day. In the morning, in the evening. Tennis hard work. Lot of running and bending for ball boy. Very hot.' It was not only the officers who played. Their wives liked a regular session on the tennis courts as well. They would play in white blouses and skirts, or even shorts and they would hurl themselves around with great abandon. To boys brought up in a Muslim culture, where women were in purdah, the spectacle must have been startling.

Respect had to be shown at all times: 'When a British officer spoke, you had to stand up. And wear a cap or a turban. This is for respect. They were very good to us, the officers. They were kind, friendly. But it was their Club. We show much respect.' It was the same in Peshawar and in every other club in India. The professionals and their staff were only servants. The distinction between masters and men was self-evident at all times.

Rawalpindi was the military headquarters of the area, a classic British colonial city of Asian bazaars with one foot in the past and a separate Cantonment with walled-in barracks, drill fields, brick houses, brick churches and brick-walled gardens. There was even a cricket pitch at the Club where leisurely matches could unfold on the green sward beneath a perfect sky. A game of sophisticated violence could be disguised by the languid air that surrounded it and by the gentlemanly enforcement of its rules. Teas would be served to the spectators and polite applause would greet the occasional boundary. It was just like England – except that rain rarely stopped play.

As the years passed, Nasrullah and Roshan continued to work at the Club, to learn what they could from watching, then to practise themselves whenever possible. Neither of them was looking beyond Rawalpindi at this stage. The height of their ambition was to follow their father and become a professional coach. Few other options were available to them. They never even considered the notion of making a living as players. Along with Hashim and Azam up in Peshawar, they had no knowledge of the commercial potential of squash. It was just a game.

Two crucial events, one at each end of the decade, helped to shape their futures. Both events took place thousands of miles away. In England, in 1930, the world's most famous squash tournament was born. There was no fanfare of trumpets; it was heralded by a simple statement in the Squash Rackets Association handbook: 'An open championship has been instituted and, for purposes of challenge, C. R. Reid has been designated open champion.' It was an announcement that was to have far-reaching implications for the Khans. The British Open had arrived, albeit in a form that would be changed before they were able to compete for the title.

In administrative terms, the game was still at an embryonic stage. The SRA had only been formed in 1928. Squash was essentially a minority sport which owed its development to the public schools, the Services and the West End social clubs. Nor was the first British Open a particularly distinguished occasion. Charles Reid of Queens Club was not an ideal nominee as champion because he was well past his best as a player. Don Butcher of the Conservative Club challenged him and beat him easily in a best-of-three match series. Because printed markers' scoresheets did not exist, the back of an envelope was used to keep the score.

Notwithstanding all this, the introduction of this de facto world championship was a vital step in the growth of the game. It provided a focus and lent an impetus. The Khans would be eternally grateful for that single sentence in the SRA handbook.

The second event which was to alter their lives took place on 3 September 1939. Britain, France, Australia and New Zealand declared war on Germany. The Second World War began in earnest. One question dominated the sub-continent: what would India do?

The outbreak of the First World War had galvanised all parts of the Empire and Dominions into action. India's war effort had been immense. All opposition to the Government ceased at the start of the war and the feelings of Indians everywhere was summed up by the Hon. Pandit Madan Mohan Malaviya, an ex-President of the Indian National Congress. He assured the Viceroy and the Governor-General that India would grudge 'no sacrifice of men and money in order that the British armies shall triumph'. There was indeed no holding back: India not only gave £100,000,000 pounds outright to Britain, she also undertook her own defence so that, for a time, there were less than 150,000 British troops in the sub-continent. Over 1,000,000 Indian soldiers went overseas to fight for the Allies.

In 1939 the situation was radically different. The British Army was still fighting a war in Waziristan and this did not stop because a larger conflict was brewing. Nor did the politicians offer unconditional support. Vociferous demands for full independence were being made by the Indian National Congress. The Muslim League was equally forceful in its claims for a separate Muslim State. These organisations did not suspend their activities because Britain had taken on the might of Germany once more.

British rule in India became increasingly precarious as she suffered setbacks in the war. On 15 February 1942, a catastrophe occurred: Singapore capitulated with a British garrison of 100,000 men, most of whom did not even fire a shot. It was the worst single military defeat the British Empire ever suffered and its effects reverberated through India. Hitherto, the British had always been invincible on their own ground. Now they had been driven to abject surrender by a Japanese army in what had claimed to be the supreme stronghold. British authority had always rested more upon prestige than anything else. The Japanese had torn it from under them.

Churchill rightly described it as 'the greatest disaster to British arms which our history records'. India herself was now faced with invasion by the victorious Japanese so it was imperative that full Indian participation in the war be secured. Buttressed by American pressure, this imperative forced the British Cabinet to change its collective mind. Churchill openly broke with his declared opinions and accepted a detailed scheme for Indian independence. He had strong personal reservations but he put them aside. Winning the war was the paramount concern and if the cost of Indian support was the granting of independence, so be it.

Under the new scheme, Indian nationalist leaders would immediately join the Viceroy's council. After the war, the provincial legislatures would elect a constituent assembly which would negotiate a treaty with Britain to settle the future form of government in the sub-continent. The Muslim provinces were to be given the right to contract out. The right to secede from the British Commonwealth and Empire was also explicitly stated.

Gandhi sabotaged the offer. At his instigation, the National Congress rejected the scheme and went on to pass a 'Quit India' resolution, urging the British to surrender all control at once. With the Japanese poised to invade, this was not one of the Congress's wiser decisions. Faced with such action, the British rounded up the leaders and put them under lock and key. Rejected in outline, the scheme lived on in essence. The major decision was made. Independence was at the top of the agenda.

War did nothing to help the game of squash. The British Open was put into mothballs for the duration and there were no advances on the organisational side. In India, too, it suffered a lull. As the global battle grew more intense, British soldiers began to look beyond the boundaries of the sub-continent. There was less emphasis on recreation at their clubs and more concern with military readiness.

Roshan Khan recalls what happened in Rawalpindi: 'The war no good for sport. People too busy. I start work as labourer. Very hard. Eight hours a day, six days a week. I work with my hands. I am tired. But every day at four or five o'clock I go back to the Rawalpindi Club. I offer them games. No shoes on my feet. I take anybody on. If I play all day, I earn maybe one rupee. When I am labourer, I get half of that in a day. Difficult time for me.'

Faizullah was coaching his sons now and they made a marked improvement. Even though still a teenager, Roshan was so outstanding that he could beat anyone at the club either at squash or rackets. He had speed, anticipation and a feline grace. His drop shot was exceptional. Nasrullah was a brilliant player, too, and was maturing into a fine coach. The one-time ball boys were now showing the British how to play the games that they had invented.

Roshan had a weakness, however. In 1941, he started to smoke and it became an addiction. He is the first to admit that it took its toll of his stamina. But with or without cigarettes, he was in a class above the very best club players.

Japan was the country which imprinted itself most deeply on Roshan's mind. His two clearest memories are of the fall of Singapore and the dropping of the Atom Bomb. 'We read in newspapers, we hear talk all the time. No war here but we know what is going on. Japan maybe invade us. Very frightening.'

The war was kinder to Hashim Khan. He had been happy to while away his time at the Peshawar Club and earn what he could. One day in 1942, his prospects brightened. The commandant of the British Air Force base in the city came to the Club to play tennis with Abdul Majeed. While they were on court, the commandant mentioned that their professional was leaving. They needed a new coach.

'Who is a good man for us?' he asked.

'Hashim Khan,' said Abdul Majeed. 'I know him well.'

It happened as easily as that. Hashim became tennis and squash professional for the Air Force Officers' Mess. Years of patient waiting were over. The job carried a wage of fifty rupees a month. Hashim was delighted. At twenty-six, he was at last able to marry and raise a family. As was the custom, he and his wife went to live in his mother's house in Nawakille.

He found his new job highly congenial. In the mornings, he would give lessons to off-duty officers. In the afternoons, he would play one practice match after another and send a string of exhausted opponents staggering off to the showers. To keep himself up to scratch, he made sure that he played other professionals. They made him run and work. Hashim was thrilled with it all: 'Where is a better job? I hope I have this life in Peshawar forever.'

In 1944 his career as a tournament player began. The Bombay Cricket Club announced a new All-of-India championship. It was open to amateurs and professionals from all over the country. Abdul Majeed encouraged Hashim to take part and the Air Force were only too glad to release him for the tournament.

The courts in Bombay were a novelty to him. They were indoor and had wooden floors. He had only ever played on cement before. He practised on wood for two days to get used to the different bounce. The other thing he had to adapt to was the presence of spectators, there being no gallery at the Peshawar courts. In Bombay he was playing in front of officers, government officials, reporters, photographers and club members. He soon came to like the applause he earned.

After coasting through the first three rounds, he met his cousin, Abdul Bari, in the final. Although they had grown up together in Nawakille, they had not seen each other for several years. Abdul Bari was the top professional in Bombay and was playing on his home court. He was the clear favourite. Bari was a big, heavy man with a powerful arm, a wide range of strokes and the best soft drop shot in the game.

Hashim was short, barrel-chested and very light. His low centre of gravity was an advantage and he scurried about the court with electrifying speed. By watching Bari's wrist movements, he could anticipate the famed drop shop and nullify it by getting to the front wall in time to put the ball away. He won the championship and then retained it for the next two years, beating Abdul Bari in the final on both occasions.

Though the development of squash was halted by the war, nothing could stop the Khans from playing. Whatever the distractions, they made time to work at their game. Hashim was the first to move into the ranks of the professionals but Nasrullah would not be long behind him. In 1943 no less a person than King George VI took an unwitting part in moulding the Khan dynasty.

The time came to replace Linlithgow as Viceroy of India. Churchill wanted to send out Anthony Eden, his Foreign Secretary and successor-designate but the King opposed the idea, arguing that Eden could not be spared from London. Churchill tried to get round the difficulty by suggesting that Eden combined the Viceroyalty with a seat on the Cabinet, using the resources of air travel to move between the two. The King found this quite unacceptable.

Churchill therefore chose as the penultimate Viceroy, Field Marshal Sir Archibald Wavell, who had been Commander-in-Chief of India. A soldier had been made caretaker until the Japanese had been defeated and the imperial structure could be dismantled. Wavell was a military man of unusual sensibility and he had political skills as well. There was another side to his character: he liked squash.

Nasrullah Khan would one day work for him.

KHANS OF PAKISTAN

When the war finally ended, the problem of India was thrown into sharper relief. The wheels of the Raj still creaked around but they would grind to a halt sooner or later. Real power no longer lay with the British bureaucracy. It resided with the nationalist politicians. Such was the rivalry between the majority National Congress, led by Gandhi and Nehru, and the minority Muslim League, led by Jinnah, that the practical issue was how Britain could get out without leaving anarchy behind. From being the glory of the Empire, India had turned into a chaotic entanglement.

The Hindu-dominated National Congress wanted to take over the whole of British India. It had many Muslim members and refused to accept that religious differences should be taken into account. The Muslim League, with its demand for a separate Muslim state called Pakistan, had consolidated its hold over most of the Muslim population.

Immediately after the war, the Viceroy, Wavell, held general elections for the central and provincial legislatures. The results showed that the Congress and the League between them controlled Indian public opinion. Wavell's next step was to try to get Nehru and Jinnah to serve together in a caretaker administration which would prepare a federal constitution to give Hindus and Muslims self-rule in their own provinces while defence and foreign policy were reserved for an all-India government. The scheme got nowhere. Jinnah was confident that if he held out long enough, he would get an entirely sovereign Pakistan.

During the summer of 1946 the enmity between the Hindus and Muslims exploded into savage riots, which by chain reaction spread right across the country. Thousands were murdered. Passions were nearing fever pitch. India was on the verge of civil war and the British administration knew that it would be unable to contain it. Desperate measures were needed.

Being a soldier, Wavell came up with a military solution. He favoured a policy of ordered retreat from the sub-continent and drew up a detailed plan of evacuation. It was rejected by the Labour Cabinet back in London and Wavell was recalled. To be the new and last Viceroy, Prime Minister Attlee made the bold decision of choosing Viscount Mountbatten of Burma, a cousin of the King. He was the first member of the Royal Family to hold such a position, albeit for a limited period.

Mountbatten arrived in India in March 1947. After assessing the situation, he concluded that swift partition was the only answer. Nehru at last agreed and joined the leaders of the Muslim League in a temporary central government to prepare the split. Everything was rushed. In June, Mountbatten announced that the date set for British withdrawal was 15 August 1947. This left only three months for the creation of two new administrations, for dividing the armed forces and for defining the frontiers of the new states. It is not surprising that dreadful mistakes were made.

The new country of Pakistan, invented in such a hasty manner, was in two separate halves. West Pakistan consisted of Sind, West Punjab, the North-West Frontier Province, Baluchistan and the former British political agencies in the northern districts. East Bengal and a great part of the Sylhet district formed East Pakistan. Between the two halves stretched almost two thousand kilometres of hostile India. It was a recipe for disaster.

One fifth of the total population of four hundred million were to be citizens of Pakistan. The rest were to remain Indians. Unfortunately, the different religious groups did not live in neat geographical areas. Even the elaborate frontiers drawn up could not match the complex Hindu-Muslim-Sikh patchwork of the population. The true enormity of Partition was borne in upon them. Within three months no fewer than seven million Muslims and five million Hindus and Sikhs were uprooted in the largest population exchange ever known.

Fears and hatreds intensified. With no authority able to hold it in check, the resentment burst into flame and massacre resulted. Stories of atrocities went from province to province and whole communities of Hindus and Muslims sought revenge. Complete trainloads of refugees crossing the Punjab were murdered. Each horror was followed by one even more appalling. India suffered destruction on a scale comparable to that which Europe had endured during the war.

The only hope of ending the nightmare was to get properly constituted Indian and Pakistani governments into power as soon as possible. Mountbatten moved with all the haste that he could. In brief ceremonies at New Delhi and Karachi, the British Raj came to an end at midnight on 14 August 1947. The union jacks were taken down for good from a thousand public buildings. It was a traumatic moment. With the loss of India, the British Empire, as governed from London, lost four-fifths of its population.

These events had great significance for the Khans. They were employed by the same British soldiers and airmen who were now pulling out. Hashim and Azam were still in Peshawar. Roshan was now helping his father at the Rawalpindi Club. And Nasrullah was still in Delhi where he had, among other things, been coaching at the Viceroy's palace which had its own squash courts. One day, the Khans were Indian citizens: the next day, they were Pakistanis.

When British withdrawal was first announced, the Pathan tribesmen on the Frontier were open-mouthed in disbelief. How could a country which had beaten the Germans and the Japanese let itself be chased out of India by a couple of Hindu lawyers? One of those lawyers, Pandit Jawaharlal Nehru, was brave enough to visit the Province in 1946, touring the Frontier with Abdul Ghaffar Khan and his brother in a forlorn attempt to persuade the Pathans to join India and thus strangle the new state of Pakistan at birth.

The tour was a complete failure and Nehru became sulky and arrogant. When he spoke at Peshawar, he got short shrift. Because he was there on political business, nobody noticed that his visit had a hidden sporting connection. The future Prime Minister of India had in fact been educated at Harrow School.

Lonely and homesick, he had written to his father in 1905 to say how dull the English boys were because 'they could talk of nothing but their games'. For one fleeting moment on the eve of Partition, Nehru linked the birthplace of squash with its second home. Without knowing it, the Asiatic Old Harrovian embodied a unique blend of the past and future of the game.

Hashim and Azam soon saw the results of the momentous changes. They were both working at the Air Force Officers' Mess now, Azam being a tennis professional there. As the British pulled out, the brothers were losing friends they had known for a long time. It was a sad occasion for them. Their jobs, however, were safe but they now coached more and more Pakistani officers. With British rule at an end, they were working for the Royal Pakistani Air Force.

Political upheaval had a detrimental effect on sport. Major fixtures in the calendar were cancelled at once. Hashim was robbed of a chance to win the All-India Professional Championship for the fourth consecutive year. Tennis players, cricketers, hockey players and other sportsmen suffered the same fate. The Pakistani military was preoccupied with establishing law and order in the new country. Hindus were fighting to get out and Muslims were struggling to get in. Bloodshed was widespread and Peshawar had its share.

Faizullah and Roshan found a similar situation in Rawalpindi. Since it was the military headquarters, there was even more action. British soldiers were packing their bags and their places were being taken by Pakistanis. Father and son survived as coaches at the Club but their work was severely curtailed. The Pakistan Army did not have much time for playing squash while they were coping with an emergency.

Roshan looks back with a resigned shrug: 'Very bad time for us. Nobody knows what is happening. Bad things happen everywhere. Not able to coach squash properly. Rawalpindi very upset.'

The confusion and uncertainty was to last a long time. The bitterness engendered by the massacres was to last much longer. It was an inauspicious start for the new state.

Nasrullah Khan was in the worst position. When the hurricane first hit the sub-continent, he was at the eye. He had been working in Delhi as a respected squash and tennis coach but his credentials suddenly became meaningless. He was a Muslim in a Hindu country. It was essential that he got to Pakistan. As long as he remained in India, his life was in danger.

There was no time for a dignified leave-taking. Nasrullah had to abandon everything and run. All that he possessed were the clothes he was wearing. The most direct way home was to the north-west but the Punjab was in a state of violent unrest. That route was already littered with the bodies of dead Muslims and Hindus. Nasrullah made instead for Bombay. It was a long, slow, tense, stuffy journey by steam train and he lived on his wits every mile of the way, fending off questions about where he was going and rebutting accusations that he was a Muslim. By way of disguise, he wore an English hat and claimed to be a Christian. There were many nerve-racking moments and he was relieved to get to Bombay in one piece.

With little money and even less time at his disposal, he had to find a means of sailing to Pakistan. When he located a passenger ship bound for Karachi, he used the last of his cash to bribe the man at the dock gates to let him through without a ticket. Then he managed to get aboard and take cover. The week-long voyage was every bit as fraught and uncomfortable as the jolting trip from New Delhi. Because he had no ticket, he had to keep out of the way of the ship's crew. He was helped by a group of fellow-Muslims who were genuine passengers. They looked after him and gave him food.

When the ship docked in Karachi, he contrived to get ashore and to stand on Pakistani soil for the first time. It was not the happiest of homecomings. He had left his country to take up a prestigious appointment in Delhi and now he was forced to sneak back. He had one item of value in his pocket: a testimonial from Wavell, praising Nasrullah's qualities as a coach and warmly recommending him. That piece of paper would in time help to get him a job in England. Meanwhile his main concern was to be reunited with his family. He had been out of communication with them and they were racked with anxiety about his safety. They were overjoyed when they saw that he had got out of India alive.

Pakistan continued to experience tremors from within and pressures from without. Its government faced massive political economic and religious problems and being split into two halves was an additional hazard. Everything about the new country had an air of impermanence about it. The administration seemed to be improvising. Boundary disputes with India eventually flared up into open warfare in Kashmir in 1948. Matters were only made worse by the death of the man who had helped to create Pakistan: Mohammed Ali Jinnah, Quaid-i-Azam, the Father of the Nation.

The Khans had no direct involvement in politics but they were bound to be affected by current events. Their country was in a state of flux and this was clearly reflected in the military institutions where they worked. They concentrated on their jobs and did their best to come to terms with the new dispensation. Gradually, things started to ease.

Their ambitions were still very much limited to their homeland. Hashim and Azam were both content in Peshawar. Faizullah and Roshan were happy to carry on in Rawalpindi. Nasrullah had no wish to return to India. None of them even thought about going to Britain and using their squash expertise as a passport.

Cricket was the main sporting contact between England and the sub-continent. The Calcutta Cricket Club had been founded, just after the MCC, in 1792. The two nations had a shared passion for the sport. The Parsee Cricket Club of Bombay had toured England as early as 1886 and during the 1890s, England actually had an Indian prince in their team – the celebrated Prince Ranjitsinhji. Playing against Australia at Old Trafford in 1896, Ranji rescued his side after two shaky starts by scoring 62 and 154 not out.

The first Test match between England and India was played at Lords in 1932. England won, as they did against subsequent Indian tourists in 1936 and 1946. While they might be masters at cricket, however, they had a much tougher time when it came to hockey or polo, and the Indian love of horses ensured that many of the English classic races were won by Indian owners.

Squash was not yet part of this international currency. Word of the exploits of the Khan family had trickled back from the Frontier with returning soldiers but that was as far as it went. In 1944, John Horry, a leading figure on the British squash scene, was stationed for a time in Bombay. There he got to know Abdul Bari, an amiable and highly courteous man. When the All-India Professional Championship was held in Bombay, Horry assisted in the running of it and he got his first glimpse of Hashim Khan who, despite taking the title, did not impress him as 'being very special'.

Conscious of the importance of developing overseas contacts in the game, Horry expressed to the squash authorities in Bombay his hope that a team of Indian professionals might visit England after the war. It was six years before that hope was partially realised. In 1950 Abdul Bari would come alone to London. His visit was the first warning shot of the Pathan invasion.

That invasion had not entered the minds of the invaders in the late 1940s. They were still going about their business in a changing environment. In 1949 the newly-instituted Pakistan Professional Championship was held in Kakul. Clubs from all over the country sent their professionals along to compete. Hashim Khan had his first competitive duel with Roshan. It was an interesting encounter and a pointer to what would follow.

Hashim was thirty-three at the time. His body had thickened slightly, his hair was receding and he sported a natty moustache. Roshan was taller, more wiry and eleven years younger. While Hashim had the bravura of a firstborn, Roshan had the reserved nature of a third son. Hashim won the contest by his usual method, his game essentially defensive, absorbing the attack of his opponent, sapping his strength with long rallies and outlasting him at the death. But Roshan played with immense flair. He was much the more stylish and attractive stroke-player, his game characterised by an uncanny control of the ball. They were indeed worthy adversaries.

The following year Abdul Bari arrived in London, funded by the Cricket Club of India, in Bombay, where he was still the professional. He made an immediate impact in his first British Open, powering his way to the final and performing creditably as he went down to the reigning champion, the elegant Egyptian, Mahmoud el Karim. Abdul Bari made many friends with his style of play. In the course of a chat with John Horry, he confided that he was not entirely happy in Bombay. Two years later, that casual conversation would bear fruit.

Bari's success brought kudos to India and corresponding irritation to Pakistan. Why was this son of Peshawar winning good publicity for the enemy? Habib Rehmatullah, the Pakistan High Commissioner in London, made a point of seeing Bari before he left. He urged the player to return to Pakistan and represent his own country. Bari was on the horns of a dilemma. He had reservations about living in Bombay but it was an excellent job. Reluctantly, he turned down the High Commissioner's offer.

It now became important to find someone else to carry the Pakistani banner in the next British Open Championship. Brigadier Engle, a retired soldier from the Indian Army, put a suggestion to the High Commissioner: 'Send Hashim Khan'. It was sound advice. The Brigadier had been Commander of the Military Academy in Kakul and he had seen Hashim play. He knew instinctively that the little man from Nawakille would be the ideal choice. The High Commissioner wrote to the government which was then based in Karachi, the temporary capital. The question was simple: 'Is Hashim Khan the best man for us?'

The government had no answer. It referred the matter to the military authorities who, in turn, contacted the Commander of the Royal Pakistani Air Force in Peshawar. Ironically, this was an Irishman called Kelly who had stayed on after British withdrawal to advise the relatively inexperienced Pakistani airmen. Commander Kelly could not give an answer. He did not play squash and was no reliable judge of the game.

Hashim was made to take on a string of Pakistani professionals so that the Commander could watch. After watching his man win all his exhibition matches, Kelly was still sceptical. He did not believe that Hashim would have the same success in England where the standard was higher. The Commander hesitated to send him. Fortunately, another member of his staff joined in the argument.

Group-Captain Raza had more knowledge of the game and had seen Hashim in action many times. He was convinced that their coach would serve Pakistan well. After all, he urged, Hashim could beat Abdul Bari and Bari was good enough to get to the final of the British Open. There could be no higher standard than that. Kelly listened intently and, in the end, agreed with the Group-Captain. Hashim would go.

Nobody had bothered to ask the man himself if he *wished* to travel to England. Hashim was very happy where he was, a married man with a growing family. Besides, he was thirty-five, well past the age when most people played their best squash. Karim was five years younger. Hashim wondered if he himself was too old to have a realistic chance of winning the British Open.

Group-Captain Raza swept his doubts aside: 'Too old to play for Pakistan?' This appeal to national pride tipped the balance. Hashim consented to go. He would represent the infant state of Pakistan and give of his best. The government provided his plane fare and the officers at the Air Force Mess clubbed together to pay Hashim's living expenses. There was no way to recoup the money. If he won the championship, he would only get fifty pounds – 'One plays this game for sport and honour'.

When Hashim Khan flew to Britain for the first time, he had a heavy responsibility on his shoulders. He carried it well. He also withstood a deal of ridicule in the early stages. When he first went on a squash court to practise, he looked a very comical figure. He was short, dumpy and balding. He had a smile as wide as the Khyber Pass. His plimsolls seemed to be much too big for him and they shrieked in pain as he zipped around the court like something out of a Disney cartoon.

Those who came to mock always stayed to applaud. Hashim Khan was the future of squash: ruthless, indefatigable and highly professional. None of his opponents ever had enough breath left to laugh at him. His beaming smile remained intact.

Hashim's first match with Karim was in Edinburgh at the Scottish Open. When they came out to knock up, they were an incongruous pair of opponents. Mahmoud el Karim, the monarch of squash in the immediate post-war era, was a slim giant of a man who always played in long white trousers. He was the professional at one of the most famous clubs in the world, the Gezira Sporting Club in Cairo. He was also heir to the mighty Abdel Fattah Amr of Egypt, who made the game his own in the 1930s. Amr Bey, as he was known ('Bey' being a title of rank conferred for his diplomatic work) won six British Amateur titles and six consecutive British Open titles.

Mahmoud el Karim restored Egyptian dominance. He was a sublime artist who seemed to stroll through a game and who could send the ball anywhere he wished with his inimitable sweeping action. There was an effortless, unhurried quality about his game. He moved with the grace of a dancer and, in Hashim's own words, 'you never hear his feet on the floor'.

Karim certainly heard his opponent's feet on the floor that day in Edinburgh. They raced at top speed over every inch of the court and one could almost smell the burning rubber. The Egyptian played with his usual rhythmical sophistication but Hashim's simple and more orthodox game won the match. The score was 9–0, 9–0, 10–8. It was a result that had many eyes popping in the squash fraternity.

Those who dismissed it as a freak occurrence were given proof that lightning could strike twice in the same place. In the final of the British Open, held at the Lansdowne Club, Hashim pitted speed, stamina and controlled aggression against the craftsmanship and precision of Karim. They were playing the same game but with different weapons – bludgeon against rapier. Hashim's victory was even more decisive this time: 9–5, 9–0, 9–0. Most players were grateful to take a point from Karim. The Pakistani had demolished him. A whole new epoch was about to begin in the game.

The Pathan invasion had started in earnest and the citadel had fallen at the first real charge. Hashim Khan was now the finest squash player in the world. He had come to London and beaten a magnificent champion with superior skill. And all because an Irishman in Peshawar was persuaded to change his mind.

It is from such slender threads of chance that the vivid tapestry of the Khan saga is woven.

CHAMPIONS

Hashim Khan returned to a hero's welcome that took him completely by surprise. It never crossed his mind that his victory could have such political significance. When his plane touched down in Karachi, the Governor-General and an official party were there to greet him. He attended a banquet in his honour and sat there smiling as praise was heaped upon him in speech after speech. He was also presented with a gold watch which had been specially engraved. Overcome with emotion, he was only able to reply with one word: 'Thanks!'

Hashim next flew by chartered aircraft to Peshawar where an even bigger reception awaited him. Five hundred guests were waiting for him at the airport. When he drove in an open car through the city, thousands of people lined the way. Schools had been closed so that children could take part in the celebrations. Hashim was touched. He knew that most of the well-wishers had never even seen a game of squash let alone played one themselves, yet they were cheering and clapping and chanting his name.

A country which was not yet five years old had its own world champion. The boost to national morale was incalculable. Hashim Khan was a name that could be waved with pride.

But it was the welcome that he got in his own village of Nawakille that meant most to him. Everybody wanted to touch and congratulate him. He was amongst family and friends. Being a Pathan meant that success was shared because part of the achievement was the source from which it came. It would be the same with Roshan, Azam, Nasrullah and, much later, Jahangir. Nawakille was the true centre of their universe.

At the age of thirty-five, an unknown squash player leaves

the obscurity of the North-West Frontier to go to London and win the world championship of one of the most gruelling games ever devised. And he does it all on behalf of a country that is still smouldering from its baptism of fire.

As the basis for a novel, it would be rejected out of hand as being too fanciful. As a television serial, it would be lucky to hold its viewers beyond the first episode. Even the Hollywood film moguls would not have risked something so patently far-fetched. Yet it conforms to Sam Goldwyn's specifications – it is a story that begins with an earthquake then works up to a climax.

Hashim Khan set off the first earthquake when he beat the Egyptian master. He would cause many other seismic disturbances along the way. At the climax of the narrative would be Jahangir Khan whose achievements would have cosmic repercussions.

But let us return to those slender threads. Because Hashim ushered in thirteen years of triumph by the Khans, it seems as if there was an inevitability about it all as if he conquered Everest, the others coming after him, roped together for safety. This is not the case at all. One of the Khans reached the summit in spite of Hashim's example and not because of it.

In 1951 Roshan Khan was still working with his father at the Rawalpindi Club. His game had matured even more and he was a convincing winner of the Pakistan Professional Championship at Kakul. Understandably, he wanted to measure himself against the new world champion but he was unable to do so. Hashim would not play him and there were no national championships in the offing which would throw the two of them together. It was highly frustrating.

Roshan was very proud of Hashim's achievement and he was inspired to emulate it. Certain that he could one day become the top player in the world, he worked harder and harder at his game. But the opportunity to tackle Hashim just never came. Out of sheer desperation, Roshan gave up his job and went off to join Nasrullah in Karachi. It was an audacious move. He had no money, no prospect of employment and no guarantee that he would get the crack at the champion that had eluded him in Rawalpindi.

Roshan had his reasons: 'Hashim is not taking part in any

championships in Pakistan. Karachi is a big city. Maybe I get the chance to go to England.' It was a long shot but worth the risk. There was a bonus: Nasrullah could coach him. His elder brother was now working in Karachi as a tennis and squash professional. Roshan could count on moral support and some of the finest teaching available.

In 1952, encouraged by his own brother, Azam was taking up the game more seriously. Roshan hoped that this year they might both compete in the Pakistan Professional Championship. But while he was travelling to Kakul, the two brothers were leaving Peshawar en route for London. It was agonising. Roshan felt that they were deliberately avoiding him. His frustration deepened.

Nasrullah came up with an idea. An ebullient man with great charm and personality, Nasrullah always had a wide circle of friends. He encouraged some of them to put up five thousand rupees if Hashim would meet Roshan in an exhibition match. The scheme attracted a lot of publicity but Hashim declined the offer. Roshan was hurt. He was soon nursing a double disappointment. While he, as national champion, was cooling his heels at home, Azam from Peshawar, and Safirullah and Mohamed Amin from Karachi were granted the trip to England that Roshan had set his heart on. It plunged him into melancholy.

Hashim and Azam were not the only players who appeared to be dodging him. Safirullah, their brother-in-law, was the professional at the Sind Club in Karachi but he would neither play Roshan nor give him access to the courts. It was the same with Mohamed Amin, the self-appointed 'number one tricky player', who was the coach at the Gymkhana Club. Roshan simply could not get on any of the best courts in the city.

The surprise is not that Roshan Khan only won the British Open once, but that he won it at all. Circumstances conspired against him. It was an uphill struggle all the way and a lesser man would have given in long before. Responsibilities weighed in upon him. Roshan had a wife and a baby son, Torsam, to support. Nasrullah could only give limited help and he had two sons of his own, Aman and Rahmat, to look after. They were dark days for that branch of the Khan family.

'I was still in Karachi. The champion. It was unfair.' Roshan remembers it all with painful clarity. 'I have no money. I was lying in the street with no house, no job, no racket, no shoes. I am Pakistan champion and I live like that. All day I help Naz with the tennis to get some money. They would not allow me to play squash. At night I used to go to open ground where they build Inter-Continental Hotel later on. I run round. Try to keep fit. Not eating properly. The position was so bad I couldn't buy a racket to practise. And if I could, they would not let me play. There was much politics against me. I told Naz, I don't think I get a chance to play Hashim or the others. Waste of time. I better go to work, some job, make money. Every day, the situation get worse. I not put up with it much longer.'

In 1953, he was on the brink of giving up squash altogether: 'It was a very near period'. Having to eke out a bare existence was demoralising for Roshan. He started to lose his appetite for the game. It seemed cruel. A country which had feted its world champion was now ignoring one of its national stars. There was nobody to whom Roshan could appeal. Just when it all looked hopeless, his brother came to the rescue. Nasrullah had a friend who took Roshan to meet an officer in the Pakistan Navy.

Roshan told his story and backed it up with a sheaf of newspaper cuttings. The officer was moved: 'I will put you in the Navy as messenger. This job is not suitable for you but I am opening the way.' The naval officer was a squash player himself and often went to the Gymkhana Club for a lesson with Mohamed Amin. When the coach rejected another challenge from Roshan, the suspicion that he was giving him the slip was confirmed.

Having joined the Navy, the messenger was summoned by the Chief of Staff. He was asked if he could really beat Hashim. Roshan was honest.

'No, sir. I am not claiming that I am going to beat him. But I want a chance to play him. Request that you press him to play me in Pakistan, or send me to England.'

'England?'

'Is best place for squash. Many good players there.'

'When is going to be next Kakul Championship?'

50

RAWALPINDI CLUB, 1932.
Lt.-Col. Remington of the Black Watch presides over this impressive display of trophies. Standing, second from the left, is Faizullah Khan; on his left is Said Ali Khan, next to whom is Abdul Majeed Khan. The bareheaded teenager standing second from the right is Hashim Khan.

RAWALPINDI CLUB, 1936.
More trophies on display. Faizullah Khan stands extreme left. Amin Khan, the marker, is on the extreme right. Nine-year-old Roshan Khan sits cross-legged on the ground.

KAKUL, December 1949.
There were Khans galore at the first Pakistan Professionals Tournament. Hashim, the winner, sits to the left of cup. Roshan, the runner-up, is beside him.

(LEFT) Faizullah Khan, father of Nasrullah and Roshan.

(ABOVE) BROTHERLY LOVE. Nasrullah (left) and Roshan Khan

AWESOME FOURSOME.
to right: Roshan Khan, Azam Khan, Hashim Khan and Jamal Din.

E) DANGER AREA. The warning on the door of the
Court at the Lansdowne Club says it all. Beware if
o on court with (left to right) Hashim Khan, Roshan
Abdul Bari, Nasrullah Khan or Azam Khan.

) DENTAL INSPECTION. Roshan Khan lost seven
– but won the match – when Azam's racket hit him
mouth during the final of the 1957 Dunlop Open.
lah examines the scars of battle.

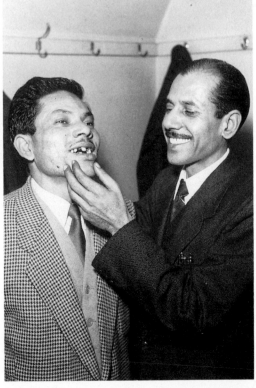

(LEFT) Nasrullah Khan practises his backhand.

(RIGHT) BRITISH OPEN, 1957. Not even the mercurial brilliance of Hashim Khan (left) could prevent Roshan from winning the title this year.

(BELOW) WHITE HOUSE MEMORIES. President John F. Kennedy gives a warm welcome to Mohibullah Khan, shaking his hand, and Roshan. The American president urged both of them to work in his country as coaches.

(FAR RIGHT) President Ayub Khan of Pakistan pins the Pride of Performance Medal on Roshan Khan. It is the country's highest award for sporting achievement.

(OPPOSITE BELOW LEFT) An early photograph of Torsam Khan and his sister.

(RIGHT) An exhausted Torsam relaxes after a match. A week later, he collapsed on court in Australia and died.

THE MAGNIFICENT SEVEN.

Outside the newly-opened PIA Squash Complex in Karachi in 1976, seven world champions line up. Left to righ Azam Khan, Geoff Hunt, Hashim Khan, Jonah Barrington, Roshan Khan, Mohibullah Khan and Qamar Zaman.

GROUP PORTRAIT.

The world's leading players in 1977. Back row, left to right: Kevin Shawcross, Roland Watson, Cam Nancarr Qamar Zaman, Gogi Alauddin, Ali Aziz, John Easter. Middle row, left to right: Murray Lilley, Rahim Gul, Rahi Khan, Hiddy Jahan, Mohibullah Khan junior, Owen Emsley (promoter). Front row, left to right: Khalifa Salem, Ge Hunt, Bill Andress, Torsam Khan, Achmed Safwat, Abbas Kaoud, Bruce Brownlee.

STARS OF THE SEVENTIES. Back row, left to right: Mo Yasin, Hisam Din, Torsam Khan, Mr Boyce of Edgbaston Priory Club, Rahmat Khan, Gogi Alauddin. Kneeling, left to right: Aman Khan, Sajjad Muneer, Hiddy Jahan.

(BELOW) The young Jahangir.

WORLD CHAMPION.
...urne, 1979. A rueful Phil Kenyon stands beside ...year-old Jahangir Khan, new World Amateur champion.

DEADLY RIVALS.
Jahangir and Geoff Hunt share a relaxed moment in Germany. On court, the mood would be very different.

BEST FOOT FORWARD.
Jahangir in tribal pose for one of his sponsors.

'Later in year, sir.'

'If you win for third time, we promise to send you to England.'

The bargain was struck and Roshan was determined to fulfil his side of it. He had at last been given a target to aim at. Hashim and Azam did not take part in the next Pakistan Professional Championship but that was immaterial.

Fired by the offer that had been made to him, Roshan won the trophy in style and took it back to Karachi for the Pakistan Navy. They were delighted. His messenger's job was cancelled, his pay was increased and he was told that, from now on, he would play only tennis and squash. It was music to Roshan's ears.

They were still prepared to send him to England but they did not have much foreign currency. How much did he need? Roshan made no demands: 'Pay my ticket and give me a little money and forget me.' The Navy took him at his word. He travelled by air to England and arrived with only five pounds in his pocket. It was the dead of winter.

Roshan was hardly well-prepared: 'First trip, I have one pair of trousers, one shirt, one pair of tennis shoes. Snowing in London – and I wear tennis shoes. People laugh. And one long overcoat borrowed from the stores, to be returned. No squash gear at all. No racket. People are saying "You will die hungry in England".'

For someone who had been basking in the warmth of a Karachi winter, it was a severe shock to the system, but Roshan survived. He was brought slap-bang up against the expense of living in Britain. By the time he had paid his landlady in advance and taken a taxi to the Pakistan Embassy, he had a solitary pound left in his pocket. He was handed over to Henry Hayman, then Secretary of the Squash Rackets Association. Hayman was shaken when he learned that the Pakistani had no equipment. He took Roshan straight off to Lillywhites of Piccadilly. They gave him shoes, socks, shorts, shirts and two rackets. The total cost was in the region of fifteen pounds.

There was no way that Roshan could pay for it. Thinking that he had travellers' cheques which he had not cashed, Hayman paid out of his own pocket. Bundling Roshan into a taxi,

Hayman then took him on a tour so that he could meet the professionals in the West End Clubs. It is at this point that another slender thread of chance appears. Abdul Bari was at the Junior Carlton Club. He had been brought over earlier in the year by John Horry, who was captain of squash at the club. When the resident pro, Bert Biddle, was forced to retire because of ill health, Horry had recalled his talk with Bari during the 1950 Open. He made an official approach and the Pakistani professional joined them in the new year.

Horry had taken a risk but it paid off handsomely. Both as a player and as a teacher, Abdul Bari was an instant success and he soon settled into the club. Roshan was thrilled to find his cousin employed there. Bari let him play at the club without paying which was highly fortuitous as money was very scarce.

Nasrullah had accompanied his brother to England. He and Roshan now tried to raise what funds they could to keep themselves going. Naz tapped a friend in Birmingham. Then there was the Embassy and the Pakistan Navy. Roshan got his expenses, which came to about four pounds a week. What happened next is one of his cherished memories: 'First tournament was Dunlop Championship. Worth five hundred guineas, very big championship. Winner would take over one hundred guineas. Slowly, slowly, I start winning. In the semi-finals, I meet Azam. Match is very tough. Because my health and the food situation is bad, I suffer. Next day both legs were sore, ankles swollen. No walk. Spent all day in my room – 23 Cranley Gardens. One day for rest. Next day I come to Lansdowne Club. Ankles still swollen so I not wear my shoes. I put on shoes without laces and press foot.'

It was hardly the way to enter into his first major final in Britain. When he walked into the changing room, his opponent, Mahmoud el Karim, was telling some reporters that he would win because he had more experience. When they came over to Roshan, he was ready with a comment: 'I heard what he said. He will get lots of trouble. Not very easy.' Roshan was as good as his word. Nasrullah helped to psyche his brother up, the adrenalin flowed and Roshan forgot all about the pain in his feet. Showing the fighting spirit of the Pathans, he won the match 9–6, 9–0, 9–1. He had defeated a former world champion and launched himself on his international career. Another Khan was at last airborne.

Hashim now had three Open Championships under his belt. In 1953 he brought Azam with him so that he could groom him as his successor. The younger brother found the training regime far too Spartan at first but he persevered. When the British Open was next held, in March 1954, Azam beat Roshan in the semi-finals before going down to Hashim in the final. It was becoming a family affair.

The two brothers were very friendly towards Roshan but they still would not practise with him. They played together so that they could discuss how to beat him. Roshan was at a profound disadvantage. The seeding was often arranged so that he had to beat Azam and Hashim in order to win. In time, when young Mohibullah Khan joined them, Roshan was up against three of them. 'I had three Geoff Hunts against me.'

One thing he did have in his favour, however, was the presence of his brother. When Abdul Bari died suddenly of a brain tumour in 1954, the Junior Carlton was left without a professional. Naz was desperate to get the job. The testimonial which he had smuggled out of Bombay now came into its own. On the recommendation of the late Lord Wavell and others, he was appointed to replace his cousin. John Horry admitted that he took a gamble because he had never met the new coach but his luck held. He was later to describe Nasrullah Khan as 'probably the greatest teaching professional to come out of the East'.

Roshan now began to divide his time between England and Pakistan with occasional forays elsewhere. Naz had a room at the club and so Roshan lived alone in his bedsitter in South Kensington. His abiding memory of England is the weather: 'Always so cold. And windy. Even cold on court sometimes. Freezing. I couldn't wait to get back to the sun. Karachi climate, very nice.'

Because the tournament circuit was still small, Roshan had to supplement his earnings by using his own teaching skills in the clubs. A normal day would begin at nine in the morning and finish at eight in the evening with time off for lunch. Roshan would expect to work with five or six members in that time and play approximately twenty-five games of squash. It kept him fit but not match fit. Though the standard was high, none of the members could test him so he was always playing below his best. It was a taxing routine and it was difficult for him to embark on his own training programme afterwards.

In 1955 he got to the semi-finals of the British Open and was beaten by Hashim in five games. In the following year, the seeding matched the two brothers in the semi-finals. Roshan beat Mohibullah in the other semi-final then took a game off Hashim in the final itself. Four members of the same family in the semi-finals – it had never happened before.

In March 1957, at his fourth attempt, Roshan was at last able to assert his supremacy. He beat Hashim 6–9, 9–5, 9–2, 9–1. After six British Open victories in a row, the old warhorse had finally been bested. He complained of cramp in his legs after the first game and that his movement was impaired. Roshan's summary of the game is somewhat different: 'I was trying to play by stamina. When I found he had lots of stamina, I played my strokes game. He couldn't get there. I took over by strokes.'

It was a popular win and Roshan played inspirational squash to achieve it. He was the only man ever to beat Hashim in the final of a British Open, and though he secured other significant victories over him, this was the one that mattered most. Two other memories make 1957 stand out as a special year for him. His second son, Hassan, was born in Karachi. And he won the Dunlop Open in spite of a spectacular injury sustained during the match.

His opponent was Azam Khan and the final was yet another tense duel between them. Roshan got the upper hand and took the first two games. Then came the drama: in the heat of battle, Azam's whizzing racket hit Roshan full in the mouth. Blood spurted everywhere and teeth dropped out on to the floor. Roshan's white shirt was a mass of red stains. A doctor was summoned from the audience to examine him. Fearing that the player might be concussed from the blow, he held up three fingers to test him.

'How many fingers have I got up?'

'Five,' said Roshan.

'That does it. You're not fit to play on.'

54

'I was only joking,' added Roshan with a painful grin.

'*Joking*! At a time like this?'

'You had three fingers up.'

'Are you sure?'

'Yes,' replied Roshan. 'And I *must* play on.'

Seven teeth had been knocked out or loosened. The game was held up for a long time. Nasrullah was on hand to give advice and he urged his brother to fight on. Roshan did just that. He lost the next two games, then staged a fine recovery to take the fifth game and the title. Photographs of the presentation ceremony show him holding the smart new briefcase he had won and bestowing a gap-toothed grin on all and sundry. He had shown immense courage as well as skill. Not even some spontaneous dental treatment could stop him from winning. Roshan explains with a shrug: 'I am a Pathan and we never give in.'

Bad luck deprived him of the chance to defend his British Open title the following year. He had knee trouble. All sports have their favourite injuries. In tennis, it is the elbow. In showjumping, it is the back. In rugby, it is the collarbone. In squash, however, it is the knee, a joint that has to absorb the most unrelenting punishment as a player twists, turns, sprints, stops, bends and stretches time and again. Roshan had problems with both knees. First the right and then the left caused him pain.

He went to have his right knee X-rayed and was told that a cartilege operation was necessary. Roshan had heard a lot about the wonders of British medicine but he was still cautious.

'Will the operation be successful?' he asked.

'Probably,' he was told.

'Will I still be able to play squash?'

'Probably.'

'At the same level?'

'We can't promise anything,' admitted the doctor. 'In this sort of case, we can't give a categorical assurance. You *might* be able to carry on and you might not.'

It was too big a risk to take. Roshan decided to put up with the discomfort. His knees continued to give him trouble. One day, some years later, he was coaching a player on court. She noticed that he was limping and asked the reason. When he told her about the history of his knee trouble, she expressed a keen interest. The woman turned out to be an orthopaedic consultant and she invited him along to her surgery. A squash player herself, she was only too ready to help a champion back to full fitness. But the consultation turned out to be more like a culture clash.

Roshan was shown into her surgery. They were alone.

'Good morning, Mr Khan.'

'Good morning.'

'I do hope we'll be able to help you,' she said briskly. 'Now – just take off your trousers, please.'

'What!' Roshan was horrified at the suggestion.

'Take off your trousers.'

'I am sorry. That is impossible.'

'Why?'

'You are a woman.'

'I am also a doctor.'

'Oh, no,' explained Roshan with an apologetic smile. 'I am a Muslim. I could not take off my clothes in front of a woman.'

'What about your wife?'

'She is different.'

'I can't examine your knee unless I *see* it, Mr Khan.'

The argument went on for some time and then a compromise was reached. Roshan agreed to roll up his trouser leg so that she could get at his knee. She used a little hammer to test his reflexes then examined the knee with great care. Her diagnosis was the same as that of the other medical experts.

'You need a cartilege operation.'

'Will it work?' he asked.

'With luck.'

'And if it doesn't?'

'Ah, well . . .'

The doctor was honest with him. She conceded that there was a risk of failure. It might not only terminate his playing days but jeopardise his livelihood as a coach. Roshan was not prepared to take the chance. What would happen if he did not have the operation? The doctor told him that he could play on but that his knee would never stand up to the intense pressures of the world circuit. His time at the top was over.

Azam, too, had retired from competitive squash by this stage. In 1962 his career came to an abrupt end when he damaged his Achilles tendon. He was to continue as proprietor and coach at the New Grampians Club in Shepherd's Bush, London. Even though he grew up in the shadow of his elder brother, his achievements were considerable. He won four successive British Opens and reached the final on three further occasions. Three months before the injury which retired him, he won the US Open in Atlantic City, New Jersey. And there were countless other wins in major tournaments around the world. The dazzling smile and equally dazzling talents of Azam Khan were known and appreciated wherever the game was played.

The family baton was now handed on to the young Mohibullah Khan, who won the British Open in 1962 by coming from behind to beat Abou Taleb of Egypt. At the peak of his success, he emigrated to America where he became the professional at the Harvard Club in Boston on the personal recommendation of President John F. Kennedy. Mohibullah and Roshan had visited Washington in 1960 and played on the Pentagon's own court. Kennedy was so impressed that he urged both of them to come to America on a full-time basis. Hashim had already led the way by accepting the offer of a job in Detroit. Two years later, fresh from his triumph in the British Open, Mohibullah followed suit.

Roshan decided against the move. Though he enjoyed the American game and won the U.S. Open three times, he preferred to return home to his family in Karachi. He felt that his primary loyalty was to the Pakistan Navy, which had rescued him in his hour of need. It was time to repay the faith they had shown in him.

Thirteen years of Khan ascendancy were over. Endless discussions have been held about who was the best of them and no firm conclusions have been reached. Hashim Khan, as the front-runner and holder of a (then) record seven British Opens, has most supporters and he was the senior player in every respect. He created Azam in his own image but there are those who feel that his younger brother was even better, more subtle, inventive, mercurial.

Roshan has no doubt that Hashim was the stronger of the two because of his ability to keep an opponent under constant pressure. Again, Hashim's consistency was daunting. Roshan himself was a player for the connoisseurs, lithe, resourceful and imaginative, a man who glided around the court with liquid grace and who always seemed to be in the right position at the right time. It is generally agreed that if he had not been dogged by injury and handicapped by clan rivalry, he would have won the British Open more than once.

Mohibullah was another superb player, robust, expressive and totally committed. He played the game as if his life depended on it and he hurled himself around the court with alarming gusto. This do-or-die attitude made for some incredible acrobatics and some grotesque facial expressions. Mohibullah Khan was a one-man firework display, an explosive mix of ferocious hitting and tireless retrieving. Wise opponents simply lit the blue touchpaper and withdrew. Pulsing with vitality and gloriously free of inhibition, he would play each point as if it were the last one on earth. He may have lacked Hashim's control, Azam's guile and Roshan's finesse but he made up for it in sheer entertainment value. Full of sound and fury, he somehow managed to convey a deep enthusiasm for the game itself. Squash was fun.

Individually, the Khans were brilliant; collectively, they were unbeatable. During their reign, they lifted the whole standard of squash and showed what could be attained by dedicated professionals who were ready to push themselves to the limit. The irony was that they reached such a level of perfection that they had only each other to play against.

Their dominance is a testimony to family solidarity, though family rivalry – as in Roshan's case – could be a disabling factor. Cynics believed that they clung too rigidly to the pecking order of the Pathan household. It was argued that Azam allowed his elder brother to win at least one of his Open titles and that Mohibullah showed the same restraint when pitted against his uncle, Azam. The Khans dispute these claims and certainly none of them did any favours on court for Roshan. They played to win. Family hierarchy may have had some influence at a subconscious level but it was never decisive.

The simple fact was that all four of them were superlative players who deserved to be world champions. They came from nowhere yet went all the way to the top. Even in hindsight, that achievement looks staggering.

Who was the greatest of the Khans? Hashim? Azam? Roshan? Mohibullah? The question continued to be asked long after their lustre began to fade. In December 1963, almost unnoticed, a new name slipped into the reckoning. Roshan was in London when he received a telegram from Pakistan. It announced the birth of his third son.

Jahangir.

NAZ

The Pathan invasion carried all before it but it must be set in context. It did not set the Thames on fire or even ignite one of the smaller tributaries. Squash was still small beer. When the Khans first descended, it was primarily a minority sport with an element of snobbery attached to it. Played in the social and services clubs, it suffered badly during the war when those institutions were depopulated. The game was further handicapped when supplies of rubber were stopped and virtually no new squash balls were manufactured. After the war, squash took time to re-establish itself and was still seen by many as a recreation rather than a real sport, a way of keeping fit for more important activities.

The game had little spectator appeal and this is borne out by the kinds of court that were constructed. Few allowed for more than a handful of onlookers. At the outbreak of war, there were twenty-seven West End clubs with facilities for squash. The average number of courts was two. After the war, several of the clubs had to close down or amalgamate, thus further reducing the number of available venues. The Bath Club in Dover Street had been destroyed by fire and so the Amateur Championship, along with other SRA events, was transferred to the Lansdowne Club in Berkeley Square.

The Lansdowne had always catered for the younger set, offering, in addition to squash, a swimming pool and a fencing salon. At the instigation of the far-sighted Lord Aberdare, a court with a large gallery had been built in 1933 and opened two years later. It had seating for almost a hundred and fifty. With standees, it had a total capacity of two hundred. The Bruce Court was thus the largest in London. It was to be an apron stage on which some of the finest dramas of post-war squash were acted out.

It was here that Hashim Khan took his first British Open title from the firm grasp of Mahmoud el Karim. On this same court, he won his six other titles and sustained his only defeat in the event at the hands of Roshan. It was at the Lansdowne that Norman Borrett, current President of the Squash Rackets Association, won his five consecutive Amateur Championships, where Gavin Hildick-Smith became the only South African champion in 1951, where Alan Fairburn, Roy Wilson and Nigel Broomfield took the title for England and where the unseeded Ibraham Amin of Egypt became, at twenty-one, the youngest player since Amr Bey to win the event.

Hundreds of famous and infamous matches were played at the Lansdowne Club. Crowds of thirty and forty thousand would troop off to watch goalless draws in the Football League every Saturday and take their discontent off to the nearest pub. Barely two hundred people would witness majestic squash played by the greatest players in the world. If a British Open champion got a mention in the newspapers, it was as much as he got. If his name was spelled correctly, it was a bonus.

Khan dominance of the game had been comprehensive but it was not reflected in massive financial reward. Apart from anything else, the competitive circuit was very limited. There were only a clutch of championships in Britain. Even with those in America, Canada, Australia, New Zealand and Pakistan, it did not add up to a lucrative income. Sponsorship had not yet entered squash in a big way. Television was only starting to hypnotise the British populace. To make a living, the Khans could not rely on their tournament winnings.

Exhibition matches were another source of income and the Khans exploited it to the full. In the wake of the 1954 British Open, Hashim and Roshan toured the country to play a series of matches. One of the venues was Millfield School in Somerset, where the headmaster made Hashim an offer that astounded him. Hearing that the champion's eldest son was a promising squash player, the headmaster offered the boy a free place at the school. Hashim could never have afforded the fees at the public school and he was overcome by this act of generosity.

Sharif Khan – the first of, ultimately, twelve children – left Nawakille to come to Millfield. The two places could not have been further apart in every way. After initial difficulties, the boy settled down well and repaid the headmaster's investment by winning several matches for the school and two British Junior Amateur Championships. Following his father to America, Sharif would later become the master of the hardball game, winning the North American Open Championship twelve times in thirteen years. Millfield gave his squash the opportunity to flower. Hashim's visit to the school was yet another example of a slender thread of chance.

The only regular source of income for the Khans was from coaching and they all worked as professionals at a club. Hashim and Mohibullah would move on to the richer pickings in America and, in time, Azam would join them. Roshan coached during his stays in England then went back to a full-time job with the Pakistan Navy. Nasrullah was the only member of the family whose coaching career kept him in England for the remainder of his life.

Arguments about the greatest player always involve the names of Hashim, Azam, Roshan and Mohibullah. When it comes to electing the finest coach, however, there is usually no dispute. One member of the family stands out from the others in this department: Nasrullah Khan – Naz.

He had an excellent role model in his father. Faizullah was respected throughout the sub-continent for his coaching techniques. Stern and demanding, but always fair, he worked diligently at every aspect of his job. Faizullah had a knack of identifying and developing whatever talent a particular player had. Naz took after his father. He was a born teacher and a supreme motivator and was still in his teens when he got his first work as a professional. Coaching all over India and Pakistan, he won golden opinions on every side. Wavell was not the only former employer to give him a glowing testimonial. Naz was special.

His first assignment was to coach Roshan. As well as honing his younger brother's game, he instilled him with confidence, fired his ambition, nursed him through moments of despair. A gracious and affable man, Naz had a gift for making friends and keeping them. It was one such friend who introduced Roshan to the naval officer and thereby changed his whole life. The two brothers set out for England for the first time in December 1953.

By an odd coincidence, it was the death of Abdul Bari – the first man to beat him in a major British tournament – which gave Naz his opportunity to work at the Junior Carlton Club in Pall Mall. He was to stay there almost nine years and consolidate a growing reputation. Like Azam, he came late to the competitive side of squash. Azam was in his late twenties before Hashim weaned him away from his tennis and put him through the tortures of his training sessions.

Both as coach and competitor, Naz was a tennis specialist and he was in his thirties before he switched decisively to squash. He was an exceptional player at both games. When he first came to England he had to pass a driving test in tennis and squash before he was allowed to coach himself. Bill Moss, the British professional tennis champion, was nominated to give him the first test and was quite bemused when Naz beat him 6–3, 6–2. In squash, too, he always looked good. He was a class performer with something of Roshan's elegance about him.

Cartilege trouble hampered his playing career but he was still able to reach two quarter-finals in a British Open, losing on both occasions to Hashim, and one semi-final, when he went down to a bouncing Mohibullah. In the 1960s he would go on to win four Open Veterans titles and to feature in two other finals. With more luck, less injury and an earlier commitment to squash, it is likely that he could have been yet another of the family world champions.

But it is as a coach that he is best known and remembered. He guided Roshan throughout the latter's career and the brothers were company for each other during their long exile from their families in Pakistan. Naz would always be in Roshan's corner during a match, advising, cajoling, warning, urging and controlling tactics. When Roshan went back to Karachi to live, he looked after his brother's family. In time a marriage was arranged between his eldest son, Torsam and Nasrullah's daughter. The family unit was bonded even more closely together.

Naz was to coach many other players but one of them was to turn into a world-beater: Jonah Barrington. On the face of it, he was a most unlikely candidate to take on the mantle of the Khans. Barrington was short, slight and very short-sighed. He had been living a life of youthful dissipation. Thrown out of Trinity College, Dublin, because he found that Guinness is good for you and much more pleasurable than studying for exams, he drifted aimlessly for a while. One day in 1962 he was at the Junior Carlton Club, watching a game of squash between two of his friends.

Naz, the resident professional, came into the gallery. He was a stocky man of medium height with rapidly thinning hair and a dark stripe of a moustache. The piercing eyes, aquiline nose and proud bearing gave him a patrician air. There was an aura about the man and Barrington sensed that he knew more about the game of squash than anyone he had ever met. Naz exuded authority.

Plucking up his courage, Barrington went over to the Pakistani and asked for some advice. He told Naz that he was very keen to improve his squash but that he lived in Cornwall, eight miles away from the nearest court in Bude. The coach heard him out then quietly passed on his counsel: 'You must bicycle to the squash court, or, if you can run, run; it is very good thing. And when you get to the court, you must practise. You must hit the ball up one side wall one hundred times. This very good thing. Then you hit ball up other side one hundred times. This very good thing. And you must skip on court. This very good thing. Very good practice. This will make you very good squash player.'

Given in his inimitable way, Naz's advice was sound. He was encouraging the young player to concentrate on the two basics of squash: fitness and ball control. Barrington acted on his suggestions and his game improved as a result. But the two of them were not destined to begin their partnership for some time yet. Indeed, Barrington's interest in the sport waned. It was revived in the summer of 1964. John Mocatta, an Oxford graduate and a very useful squash player, was on holiday in Bude. He rang the family home in Morwenstow to ask if Nick Barrington would give him a game. As his brother was out,

Barrington deputised for him and was duly thrashed on court. Afterwards, his opponent asked him what he was doing with himself.

Barrington admitted that he was unemployed and probably unemployable. Undeterred, Mocatta told him that there was a clerical job going at the Squash Rackets Association. Did the idea appeal to him? Barrington was more than interested. Six weeks later, he got a letter from John Horry, then Secretary of the SRA. He landed the job and moved to London in September. Until the end of the following year, the future world champion worked as a general dogsbody in a Regents Park office the size of a glorified broom cupboard. When there were three people in there, it was like Piccadilly in the rush hour.

John Horry certainly helped to lubricate the wheels of the Khan dynasty. He was instrumental in bringing Abdul Bari to England, he gave Nasrullah the job at the Junior Carlton and he brought the coach together with his prize pupil. A small, round, bespectacled man from the colonial office, Horry had an encyclopaedic knowledge of the sport and he *was* the SRA for many years. Squash owes him an enormous debt and the Khans would want to throw in their vote of thanks to someone who was a continuous help to them.

Barrington's early attempts to develop his squash in London were disappointing and he became disheartened. Horry approached Naz and asked him to help the budding player but the Pakistani had just moved to the Lansdowne Club and was only allowed to coach members. With an income of a mere six hundred pounds a year, Barrington could not afford to join the club. His squash improved at a stroke, however, when he exchanged his glasses for contact lenses. The whole game suddenly came into focus and he devoted more and more time to it. He also became a fitness fanatic.

Though Naz was not officially able to coach him, he did feed him with a regular stream of advice. They came into contact through the SRA and through a friend who used to take Barrington to the Lansdowne Club to play as a guest. Desperate to learn, Barrington plied Naz with questions. Pleasant, courteous and eager to help, the coach gave him all the answers. The relationship between them slowly deepened. It would eventually become a kind of symbiosis.

Naz and his new charge had much more in common than was apparent to the naked eye. The coach was first and foremost a Pathan, a man who had learned to adapt his warrior instincts to a sport. Barrington was the son of a soldier. Major Charles Barrington had actually served on the North-West Frontier at one time and he had a great respect for the Pathans. His son inherited his military cast of mind and came to see squash as a war waged with a racket. This attitude blended perfectly with that of Naz. Both men understood the importance of winning at all costs. Losing was dishonourable. Whatever else he was going to be, Barrington would never continue the tradition of the gallant British loser.

There was another linking characteristic. Both men were obsessional. Once they got involved in something, they gave it their full and undivided attention – they were hundred per centers. Naz took a death-or-glory approach while Barrington had true Celtic zeal. Though he was born in Cornwall, the player had an Irish father and a Welsh mother, two parents who equipped him with a serviceable amalgam of blarney and *hwyl*.

Naz and Barrington were kindred spirits, two lonely souls in search of friendship, drawn to each other with such intensity that they became almost like father and son. Each was a perfectionist who set his sights on the top. Nothing less was good enough. Naz expected unquestioning obedience and it is to Barrington's credit that he was able to accept the strict regimen that was imposed upon him. In the Swinging Sixties, while the rest of London was letting its hair down, the player led an existence of monastic denial: no cigarettes, no drink, no sex, no distractions of any kind. It was a huge price to demand of healthy, single young man of twenty-five.

But the end justified the means. To become a world champion, Barrington was ready to make super-human sacrifices. In the dictates of his coach, he saw a way to achieve his goal: in the progress of his protégé, Naz saw the chance of fulfilling his own blighted ambitions for sporting success. Together, they were irresistible.

In the autumn of 1965, however, Barrington was not yet on the threshold of victory. He was being held back by circumstance. Naz therefore got together with Nick Barrington to organise a collection among friends to raise the thirty pounds membership fee to join the club. As soon as the player was entitled to come to the Lansdowne on his own account, the coach got to work on him with a vengeance.

Naz took his pupil on court to make a proper appraisal. They played two games. Naz won the first with ease but Barrington came back at him in the second. Forty-five years old and slightly arthritic, the coach decided against a third game – 'I have seen enough'.

What he had seen was a player with obvious weaknesses. Barrington's technique was poor, his choice of options was sometimes naive, his tactical sense non-existent. Yet there were visible strengths as well. He had an infinite capacity to keep the ball in play, a willingness to run himself into the ground and a competitive streak that would simply not let him give up. The weaknesses could be eliminated; the strengths could be enlarged. Here was the ideal platform on which a world champion could be built.

Naz was a realist. His finest pupil to date was his brother, Roshan, a player who could swoop and wheel and dive like a bird on the wing, a magician with a bewildering array of trick shots. Barrington could never be cast in the same mould. He had to beat his opponents by hard graft rather than by intuitive genius. He had to develop a physique and a stamina able to cope with the outrageous demands made on it by his determination to win. Only when he was fitter and faster than everyone else, could he bring them all tumbling down around him.

Barrington was urged 'to devil up your muscles'. He was already doing a lot of running and Nasrullah encouraged him to do more and to take longer strides, as if reproducing the long last lunge for a ball on court. The coach also introduced him to weight-training and this soon paid dividends. Inevitably, there was a vast amount of practice on court. Naz often made him work on his own because it developed self-discipline.

The coach explained technique and lectured on tactics. He

taught Barrington how to read an opponent's game and how to exploit it at its most vulnerable points. He advised him not to play for four or five days before a tournament: 'You must be hungry like a lion without a good meal.' It was common sense. When Barrington ignored the advice, it almost cost him a British Open title.

The raw amateur who had been trounced by Mocatta in Bude was now an accomplished player. In December 1965, in his first British Open, he was good enough to beat the talented Welshman, Denis Hughes, in the first round. In the quarter-finals, he lost to Tewfik Shafik of Egypt after having led in every single game. Defeat had a sobering effect. Barrington gave up his job at the SRA to dedicate himself to squash. To keep the wolf from the door, he took on a series of part-time jobs – as a private tutor, a milkman, a dishwasher and nude model at an art school.

Naz worked on him in earnest but his arthritic knees prevented him from giving a practical demonstration of match play which would force Barrington to think and act under pressure. It was Michael Oddy, the Scots player, who suggested a possible source of help: Azam Khan. In the spring and autumn of 1966, therefore, Barrington arranged to play Azam at his club, the New Grampians, which was in a subterranean grotto in Shepherd's Bush. It was an educative experience.

Azam was past forty and retired from competitive play but he was still far too wily and strong for Barrington. The younger player was led through a torture chamber and invited to test every piece of apparatus. Physically, it was agonising. Spiritually, it was lowering. Barrington was shown that he still had much to learn. He applied himself well but he still could not get the better of the astonishing Azam. What he did take away from the sessions was a knowledge of where not to hit the ball, how to defend under extreme stress and how to punish an opponent without remorse.

Naz had got him superbly fit. Azam applied the finishing touches. The supreme test came in December 1966, at the next British Open. Abou Taleb, the defending champion, was firmly ensconced as favourite. All went well until Barrington's preparation hit a rocky patch. Forgetting Naz's warning, he played practice matches with Azam up until the start of the championship and was slaughtered on six consecutive days. In a fit of depression he considered pulling out of the Open altogether. How could he be expected to beat Taleb when he could hardly take a point from a retired player in his forties?

Azam dispelled this defeatist talk. He knew all the players in the competition and was certain that Barrington could beat them: 'I know their standard. You just keep running and get the ball back. You win, you see. You do what I tell you, you play your game, you see what happen.' Azam had watched Taleb playing at the New Grampians on the eve of the Open. While other onlookers had been dazzled by the world champion's wizardry, Azam noted that his movement was slower and that he sometimes had to push off the front wall to get back to the centre of the court.

Naz reinforced Azam's words. Taleb was not the force he had been. He had put on three inches around the waist since the previous year. Naz learned this from the Fred Perry people who supplied Taleb with his shorts. He listed the Egyptian's weaknesses and told Barrington how to play on them. The two Khans restored his confidence and assured him that he had an excellent chance of success. Azam even predicted how the match would go: 'He play winner, you return winner. He play winner again, you return winner again – Taleb hit tin, that will happen.'

Miraculously enough, it did. Abou Taleb was a fearsome opponent. It had fallen to him to end the dominance of the Khans in 1963. He might have won the previous year if he had not allowed complacence to creep into his game. He did everything but beat Mohibullah Khan, having three match balls in the fourth game of the final. Abou Taleb's real name was Abdelfattah Ahmed Aboutaleb but everyone shortened it for convenience. A solid man of middle height, he was a master of stroke-play and went into the championship with an unbeaten run that had lasted four years. He boasted that he had come to take his fourth successive British Open title.

In the first round, Barrington had a testing match with Mike Corby who was to replace Jeremy Lyon as his closest British rival. In the quarter-finals, he came up against Taleb. It was a classic confrontation: ambitious newcomer against proven champion, enthusiasm against experience, stamina against skill. The marker for the game was Nasrullah Khan so Barrington would get no help from him during the conflict. Whenever he was officiating, Naz was scrupulously fair to both players.

What Naz had done was to forewarn his pupil against Taleb's gamesmanship. The Egyptian told the staff on reception at the Lansdowne that he was going to put his opponent out of his misery early on. Barrington was not dismayed. Nor was he rattled when Taleb used the knock-up to play to the gallery, using his full compendium of flashy shots and drawing applause at will. Acting on Naz's advice, Barrington simply kept his head down and showed no emotion at all.

When the first game began, Taleb carried on in the same cavalier mode, trying to wipe out his opponent with a series of brilliant shots. But Barrington somehow kept the ball in play. Before Taleb knew what was happening, he had lost the game 9–4. It was the same story in the second game, which Barrington won 9–1. Taleb then woke up to the fact that his title was being wrested from him by a comparative novice. His approach changed at once. He intended to win by fair means or foul. What happened next had as much to do with the Marquis of Queensberry Rules as with squash. Taleb set out to blast Barrington off the court.

The challenger was subjected to the most severe physical intimidation. Taleb elbowed him, shouldered him and drilled the ball straight at him. He even hit Barrington with his racket and knocked him over. What was even more disturbing was that he at last began to play some exquisite shots. Barrington was bullied and bruised but he stuck to his task manfully. Never once did he respond to violence with violence. His self-control was remarkable.

Taleb took the third game 10–8 but he had alienated the spectators completely. All sympathy shifted to Barrington. How long would he be able to withstand the blitzkrieg? Taleb's rough-house tactics continued in the fourth game. Barrington was now almost desperate. Then he pulled a superb shot out of the hat – a backhand volleyed drop shot from the back of the service box off what had looked like a perfect drive. It revived him and demoralised Taleb. Barrington surged through to lead 8–5. Taleb asked for a let on match point but Naz did not even refer to the referee. He barked 'no let' and the name of Jonah Barrington went into history.

It was a magnificent victory, all the more so for the way in which it had been achieved. The Bruce Court erupted with delight. They knew that they had seen the next Open champion in action. Barrington did not disappoint them. He beat Ibrahim Amin in the semi-finals then won the final 3–1 against Aftab Jawaid of Pakistan.

Britain had a new sporting hero. The first world squash champion from the home countries since the war. After twenty-eight long and frustrating years, Britain had at last produced a player capable of beating the pride of Egypt and Pakistan.

Barrington took on his new role as if it was something that he had been rehearsing all his life. He also paid tribute to Naz. Without the help and guidance of his coach, he would never have got where he did in such a short space of time. Azam, too, was given his share of the credit. It was a joint effort.

Jonah Barrington was the British Open Champion. The Khans had one hand on the trophy yet again.

RISING STARS

While Naz and Azam were busy in England, the other members of the Khan dynasty were not idle. Hashim and Mohibullah were professionals on the other side of the Atlantic. Both entered regularly in the North American Open Championship, an event that was inaugurated in 1966 when the U.S. Open and the Canadian Open were combined. Sharif Khan, Hashim's Millfield-educated eldest son, was starting to catch the eye as a hardball expert. His younger brothers, Gulmast, Aziz and Liaquat, were all working hard at the game.

Roshan was still coaching at the Fleet Club in Karachi on the two courts which had been purpose-built in 1965. The shrewd father was also passing on his knowledge to his teenage son, Torsam, who was showing flair as a shot-maker. His brother, Hassan, was also old enough to be taught the game but the baby of the family, Jahangir, was ruled out as a potential player. He had been born with a hernia problem and doctors had warned that he would not be able to take part in any violent exercise.

In the latter half of the sixties, the family was living in the Abyssinia district of Karachi, a deprived inner city area with conditions that could rival Nawakille. The houses had once been used as barracks for British soldiers and they were very basic. A few rooms would serve a large family. Water was obtained by digging a well nearby. An open sewer ran through the area. When the rain came in through the roof, the occupants used to take their cots into a corner to keep themselves dry, hitching up their clothes to keep them out of the puddles.

It was the home in which Roshan was to live for a quarter of a century. Even when he was world champion, he could not afford better accommodation. Since he was looking after Nasrullah's family as well, there would be as many as ten or eleven under the same roof, all sharing the one latrine. In years to come, Roshan would suffer acute embarrassment when old friends from the squash world visited Pakistan. Instead of being able to invite them to his home, he had to make an excuse and arrange to see them at their hotels.

Nasrullah's sons, Aman and Rahmat, had almost been born on a squash court. Their parents occupied a house adjacent to the court at the college in Karachi where Naz coached. They grew up with the sound of a bouncing rubber ball in their ears. Both boys could use a racket before they mastered a knife and fork. Like their father, they first turned to tennis and each of them won national honours.

In 1964 Aman took the Pakistan grass-court singles title. Three years later, he won the national hard court singles title as well as the doubles title, with Saeed Mir. In 1967 Rahmat became Pakistan Junior hard court champion and shared the doubles crown with Meer Muhammad. Aman also won the men's singles title in the KMC Club Tennis Tournament two years running. His prowess was rewarded by a place in the Pakistan Davis Cup team that went to India.

Aman and Rahmat were products of the Coaching Scheme organised by the Pakistan Lawn Tennis Association. In the early days, they also profited from their father's advice. While he was away, it was Roshan who nurtured their considerable talents at racket sports. In April 1970, they set out for a six-month stay in England. Aman was then twenty-two and Rahmat was twenty. Their apprenticeship was over. It was time to widen their horizons.

Their father sent out their PIA flight tickets with Jonah Barrington who was due to participate in the Pakistan Open before going on to Teheran with Aftab Jawaid to play some exhibition matches. Aman was in Putnah, representing his country in a Davis Cup match against India. When he returned to Karachi, he and Rahmat went on to join Barrington in Iran before flying back with him. They revered the English player who had become an honorary member of the clan. Friendly and helpful, he made a generous contribution towards their travelling expenses.

Barrington had built up a formidable record and reputation. Three weeks after winning the British Open in 1966, he had taken the British Amateur title, beating two powerful Australians, Ken Hiscoe and Dick Carter, in the process. He thus became the first player since Amr Bey to win both events in the same season. He set himself very difficult targets. Between December 1967 and February 1969, he lined up no fewer than eight Herculean labours for himself.

There was the British Open to start the sequence off, the British Amateur in January 1968, the Egyptian Open in March, the South African Amateur Championship in July and the Australian Amateur in August. Next on the list were second cracks at the British Open and British Amateur, followed by the World Amateur Team Championships and, in February 1969, the World Amateur Individual title. Most players would not chalk up these successes in the whole of their career. Barrington proposed to bag them within fifteen months.

He duly ticked off six of his targets but the Australians tripped him up on the last lap. The burly Cam Nancarrow beat him in the 1969 British Open and Geoff Hunt ousted him in the World Amateur series. Barrington was bitterly disappointed. He felt that he had thrown away his chances of the world title with some highly uncharacteristic lapses at a critical stage of the match. Instead of ending his amateur career on a high note, he was in a mood of utter dejection. At a press conference held at the Lansdowne Club the next day, Barrington announced that he was turning professional and then made two symbolic gestures. He 'coached' Naz for a guinea and he sold a racket to Rex Bellamy of *The Times* for a shilling. There was no turning back now. He had burnt his boats.

The man with whom Aman and Rahmat Khan travelled in 1970 was thus the world's first and only full-time itinerant professional. Having won almost everything possible, he now set himself the slightly more difficult task of changing the whole face of the game. It was a propitious time for the Khans to arrive. Many radical changes would take place on the squash scene over the next decade.

Nasrullah had now left the Lansdowne and taken up an appointment at the Edgbaston Priory Club in Birmingham. Set in a leafy suburb of the city, the club had several tennis courts and ten squash courts. It was one of the finest and longest established clubs in the Midlands. Nasrullah and his two sons lived in Melton Drive, only a short walk from his place of work. Aman and Rahmat immediately sprung into their own training programme on the tennis courts under the supervision of their father. Naz made sure that they did not neglect squash. One of his main innovations at the club was to persuade many of its tennis players to take up squash in the winter months.

Birmingham was on another planet to Karachi and it took the two brothers some time to adapt. They were helped by the fact that their father had been in the country for almost twenty years, and by the friendship of Barrington who was also based in the area. It was a particular thrill for them to see Wimbledon for the first time. Tennis was their top priority but they came to realise that they would have to concentrate on squash if they intended to make a living in Britain. Short enough already, the tennis season here was often curtailed by bad weather whereas squash could be played all the year round. It was cheaper to play and easier to learn and teach.

Nasrullah was a kind and loving father but he was far from indulgent. He believed in pushing his sons as hard as he pushed himself. His schedules were demanding and left little time for any social life. Barrington had found this out. Naz had drummed into him the importance of concentration on the job in hand. All distractions had to be avoided because they would weaken his resolve. Psychological strength was a vital part of his armoury.

Sex was forbidden. Apart from the emotional disturbance it would cause, there were the physical effects. Naz argued that it somehow damaged the knees. Barrington remained celibate in the early days but felt the need for female companionship in time. On one occasion, he made the mistake of taking a girlfriend along to the Lansdowne Club. While he played a game with Denis Hughes, the girl watched from the gallery. Naz soon joined her. The two of them had an earnest discussion and Barrington found that he had just lost a girlfriend. His coach had explained to her that the player could never fulfil his ambitions as long as she was around. Barrington was really angry with Naz for the first time but it made no difference.

Nasrullah's feelings towards Barrington were ambivalent. He basked in the player's successes yet felt resentful when the game took him abroad for long periods where he was out of reach and beyond control. What Naz relished was the daily contact with Barrington, to act as his Svengali and dictate his whole performance. As a coach and a mentor, Naz was in a class of his own and his insight into the game of squash was astonishing. He loved his friends and was delightful company. But there was a possessive streak in him and this was one of the reasons why his partnership with Britain's best player foundered.

In the summer of 1970, Jonah Barrington became involved with a married woman. Madeline Ibbotson was the wife of Derek Ibbotson, former world mile record-holder and a symbol of Yorkshire grit. The couple lived in Huddersfield with their three daughters. Barrington met them in Sheffield through a mutual acquaintance and they all went for a training run together in Graves Park. Madeline, former British 800 metres indoor record-holder, was impressed by the way that Barrington kept up with them. He became a friend of the family and occasionally stayed at the house.

The Ibbotsons seemed to have a secure and happy marriage. It was only later that Barrington learned that there were difficulties. He then made his own feelings known and he and Madeline were drawn to each other. After much heart-searching, she left her husband in January 1971 and travelled south to meet Barrington at the Lansdowne Club. Unfortunately, they were spotted by a journalist who began to probe and speculate. Within twenty-four hours, the *Daily Mail* let the world in on their secret: 'Ibbotson's Wife Says: I Love Squash Star.' The rest of the media were soon pursuing them like a pack of beagles. At a time when they most needed privacy, they were front-page news.

Nasrullah reacted to it all with horror. As an orthodox Muslim, he took a very dim view of the relationship. In his culture, such things did not happen. Women were subservient. A Pathan wife could never leave her husband because she was bound to him for life. As a friend, Naz felt profoundly betrayed because all his dire warnings had been ignored. Barrington had let the worst possible thing interfere with his squash: a love affair. Naz was shocked. In his mind, he was another injured party.

Aware of the bond between coach and player, Madeline made an effort to get to know Nasrullah but it came to nothing. When she first met him at the Edgbaston Priory Club, he was cold and offhand with her. She tried to explain that, as an athlete herself, she understood Barrington's training commitments but Naz would not listen to her. There was an instant personality clash. He resented her and she could find nothing appealing about him. It was only a matter of time before the relationship between the two men deteriorated.

In the summer of 1971, Barrington and Madeline set up home together in a flat in Solihull because the West Warwickshire Squash Club had the foresight and generosity to offer him free training facilities. Living so close to Naz did not endear the couple to him. Rahmat Khan remembers an incident at Edgbaston Priory. Naz was in the bar, smartly dressed as usual. Barrington came in with Madeline. He was wearing an old raincoat and baggy trousers. The couple were off to the cinema. Naz flared up and grabbed Barrington by the lapels. 'Look at you!' he said. 'Look at the state you're in!'

Matters were complicated by the fact that divorce proceedings dragged on so slowly. It would be two years before they could marry. In the interim, they had problems. Feeling constricted at home in Melton Drive, Aman Khan came to stay with them for a weekend and remained there for six months. It says much for Barrington's notion of hospitality that he let Aman live with them during this sensitive period. Inevitably, it gave more grounds for complaint to Naz.

The rift steadily widened. A measure of the gap between coach and player was seen at the British Open in February 1972. The event was held at Abbeydale Park, Sheffield, the venue where Barrington had lost to Nancarrow in the 1969 Open. He was determined to succeed this time and battled through to the final. His opponent was Geoff Hunt, the deadly rival with whom he played so many epic matches over such a long period. The Australian was in good form and prime condition. It was always going to be a close match.

The final swung first one way and then the other. At one stage, Barrington went for almost half an hour without scoring a point but he hung in there somehow. When he was 7–0 in the fifth game, even his most zealous fans were writing his chances off but he fought back to produce yet another of his now famous escape acts. The final score was 0–9, 9–7, 10–8, 6–9, 9–7. He was justified in feeling pleased with himself. But he got no hug of congratulation from Naz. Eyes aflame with anger, the coach grabbed him by the shoulders: 'You were so *slow* in the squash court!'

When Barrington later went into the bar for the pint of beer he had promised himself, Madeline had it waiting for him. As she handed it over, Naz glared in disapproval. Later on, the coach began to drink himself which was most untypical. The more he had, the more bellicose he became. It was very different from the euphoria which had surrounded Barrington's first Open Championship win.

That Naz could still work his magic was shown during a match the same year against the same opponent at the same venue. Hunt was at his best and Barrington had to fight for his life on court. Naz studied the Australian carefully then gave his player some shrewd advice: 'All right, he is fit, his legs are very strong. I see that. But maybe his arm is not so strong. Lob to his backhand. Make him stretch up. This is what you must do. Keep pressure on his arm. And put the ball down the right-hand wall. I know Hunt. He does not like to use his forehand volley too much.' Barrington did as he was counselled and it paid off. Though he was 7–2 down in the final game, he maintained the pressure on Hunt's arm and his opponent eventually suffered from cramp in his hand, yielding the match 7–9.

Afterwards, they went off to a restaurant to celebrate and Barrington admitted that he had been struggling so much in the match that he had sought divine assistance: 'I kept thinking to myself – "Come on Naz's God. Help me!" And Allah did.'

Through the person of Nasrullah Khan, Allah weighed in with some aid on other occasions, one of the most notable being early in 1974 not long after Barrington's defeat in the British Open at the hands of Mo Yasin. The player applying the pressure this time was Ken Hiscoe. Even on the familiar Court 8 at Edgbaston Priory, Barrington was rather at sea.

Rahmat watched the proceedings with growing discomfort. He had great respect and affection for the British player and did not want him to take another hammering. But Hiscoe was in a punitive mood and kept his man under constant attack. Rahmat became so upset by it all that the man sitting next to him asked if he had been taken ill. It was an example of how involved the young Pakistani was in the game. He could not bear to see a player whom his father coached taking such a beating.

Slipping out of the court, he ran to the bar to find Naz and begged him to help Barrington. His father was reluctant at first but saw how distressed his son was. Naz duly repaired to the court and was in time to boost Barrington's morale and alter his tactics. After making all the running, Hiscoe was overhauled by the resurgent British player. Thanks to Naz – and Allah – Barrington somehow came back from the dead to snatch victory. Rahmat was delighted. His action had saved the day. Naz had not wanted to watch the match but his son's intervention was decisive. When they worked as a team, Barrington and the coach were well-nigh invincible. It was just like old times – for a short while. But the differences remained.

During these years, Aman and Rahmat switched over to playing squash and made an immediate impact on the circuit. A source of income was the first necessity and both found jobs as club professionals. Aman worked at the Wimbledon Badminton and Squash Club – an ironic venue in view of his passion for tennis – while Rahmat coached at the Lansdowne. As in the cases of Nasrullah and Roshan, they found it difficult to coach and play at the highest level. The ability range of their pupils was very wide and they were forced into playing 'customers' games'. After six or seven hours on court with everything from duffers to county standard diehards, it was not easy to find the incentive to train on their own account.

They were soon joined by another member of the family. Torsam Khan. Groomed by his father, he was keen to gauge his potential in the cauldron of British squash. The brothers were overjoyed to see their cousin. When the three of them were together, there was always a torrent of laughter going on. Like most Pathans, they were all handsome, virile and bubbling with natural charm. It was only a matter of time before they set female hearts fluttering at their respective places of work.

Aman was the oldest. He had a round, pleasant face that was set off by a bushy moustache and eyes that twinkled with an impish sense of fun. His manner could be conspiratorial at times but he was already an acute observer of the squash world. Barrington often used him as a sparring partner and took him abroad to play in exhibition matches. Aman was more than capable of taking a game off the champion but was roundly chastised if he did so during an exhibition.

Rahmat was tall, slim, elegant and urbane. A keen sense of humour kept an almost permanent smile on his lips but there was a serious side to him as well. His moustache gave him a raffish appeal and there was a touch of Omar Sharif about his good looks. When he went to Australia in September 1972, his trainer, the celebrated Aub Amos, summed him up succinctly:

> 'I've seen the best players in the world and Rahmat is the prettiest. He moves around the court like a ballet dancer and he can play like a tiger. Rahmat will be one of the most stylish players in the world in three years. And I have seen the best in Dardir and Abou Taleb . . . They are beautiful ball players but Khan's execution of shots and freedom of movement ranges between power and delicateness.'

Rahmat had gone down under to compete in the Australian Professional Men's tournament. He met the boisterous Len Atkin in the final and went down to the bruising tactics of the local boy. It was the first time Rahmat encountered what he felt to be a dirty player of this kind. His rhythm was destroyed and he had no opportunity to demonstrate the touch play which had so impressed Amos. During his training sessions, he was made to run along the beach, a technique he would later apply to Jahangir.

Torsam, the shortest of them, was a frank, open, happy-go-lucky extrovert with immense bounce. Slim but well-muscled, he had a thick moustache, expressive eyebrows and features that were always animated. Torsam quivered with vitality. Unhappily, it sometimes spilled over in the wrong direction as his temper got the better of him and he began to acquire a reputation for belligerence on court. In fact, he was a superb touch player with enough ability and vision to take him right to the top. But there was a question mark over his stamina. It was a weakness that was not fully explained until his sudden death. Torsam kept it bravely hidden behind a broad grin and a determination to live life to the full.

Hiddy Jahan was another monstrously talented Pathan who came to Britain in 1970. An astute judge of his fellow-players, he had the highest regard for Torsam: 'We were very close friends. He was a wonderful person and a wonderful player. But for his disability, Torsam could have been world champion. He was that good. His racket work was brilliant. He could send a man the wrong way with a flick of the wrist. He always hit the ball one hundred per cent in the middle of the racket. A touch player of real class. The way to beat Torsam was to tire him because he wasn't strong. So you ran round him to get everything. Most European players went for his body and got a let. This gave Torsam a rest. This is why he often thrashed players who were stronger than he was. They let him off the hook.'

When Aman moved on from Wimbledon, Torsam took over as coach. He was popular with the members and did his job efficiently but his mind was always on the tournament circuit. He longed to devote himself full-time to the game so that he could put the Khan game back on the major trophies again. What people admired about him was the fact that he was fearless and outspoken, on and off court. Older followers of the sport could see a resemblance to Roshan in his quicksilver stroke-play but they did not recognise the father in the son's occasional lapses into more physical tactics. Roshan's court behaviour had been exemplary. Torsam, the former Pakistan under-sixteen champion, was to carve out his niche in the game. In his day, he could test any player in the world.

81

In the early seventies, Aman, Rahmat and Torsam were rising stars on the squash scene. Their time had not yet come but they resolved that it would. Jonah Barrington was still supreme, the winner of six British Opens and a host of other major titles, an iron man who single-handedly held off the threat of the Pakistanis, the Egyptians and the Australians. No domestic player could trouble him. The last Briton to get the better of him was Jeremy Lyon in 1966. It would be almost twenty years before Mark Maclean repeated the feat.

Barrington had won the 1973 Open by defeating Gogi Alauddin, the Punjabi pipecleaner, in straight games. Nobody realised at the time that it would be the last major Open title that he would win. Even at thirty-three, he looked set to extend his rule for some time. His downfall came in February 1974 in the Benson and Hedges British Open at Abbeydale. The executioner was Mohamed Yasin of Pakistan, a seasoned veteran with old scores to settle against Barrington who had always beaten him previously.

Mo Yasin was a short, springy individual with George Robey eyebrows above a rather morose countenance. Sturdily built and fast as a cat about the court, he was an excellent shot-maker with a good touch. He had none of the family advantages of the Khans and was for a time in the shadow of his relative, Aftab Jawaid. Yasin was a bounty hunter, a man who thought on his feet and took his few chances when they came along. He always shot to kill.

Barrington was not at his best but he still expected to win. Neither he nor anyone else imagined for a moment that Yasin could actually stop him from progressing to the semi-finals. But the Pakistani was fuelled by something greater than personal ambition: patriotic fervour. If Barrington won another title, he would equal Hashim Khan's record of seven British Opens. That was sacrosanct. Yasin set out to preserve that record and did far more. He not only demolished the British player, he signalled the end of his psychological ascendancy in the sport. Their quarter-final was indeed laden with significance.

Barrington won the first game without difficulty but he was upset when there was no sign of Nasrullah at the interval. Yasin had voluble support from a large Pakistani contingent who threw a cordon around him to keep Naz at bay. To Barrington's dismay, his coach did not try to break through that cordon. Having lost the second game, Barrington sacrificed the third when he hit a backhand out of court on his own game ball. Even though he was 2–1 down, most people felt that he would recover and come through. He had done his Houdini impression against finer players than the Pakistani.

But Yasin had the bit between his teeth. A rough, tough customer with an uncompromising style of play, he had already shown his readiness to use intimidatory methods. In the two previous games, he went straight for Barrington's back with his knee and hit him five times with the ball. Scenting victory, he combined these terror tactics in the fourth game with some excellent squash and shut his opponent out. The final score was 1–9, 9–4, 10–8, 9–2.

Visibly distressed by the result, Nasrullah was in tears at the end of the match, knowing that a golden era had come to a close. Yet he had not been there when Barrington needed him most. For reasons of his own, Naz had not forced a way through the protective cordon. Barrington felt deserted. The coach's advice might not have altered the result of the match but it would have been helpful and supportive. What happened at Abbeydale was yet another illustration of how far apart from each other the two of them had drifted.

There was an odd symmetry about it all. Barrington had leapt to prominence by defeating a reigning champion in the quarter-final of a British Open. The same fate had now befallen him. In both cases he faced ebullient players with the instincts of born streetfighters. Against Abou Taleb, he had all the answers. Against Mo Yasin, his resources had been inadequate.

Jonah Barrington was no longer the man to beat. The Khans were given a new target: Geoff Hunt.

THE NEW ORDER

Geoff Hunt was anything but a stereotypical Australian. Born down under of English parents, he was a quiet, composed, self-effacing man with the easy nonchalance of a true amateur. There was nothing brash or bolshie about him – not the faintest whiff of Crocodile Dundee. He valued his privacy. Hunt was so reserved at times that it bordered on diffidence. Though he was a ferocious competitor on court, his conduct was always impeccable: no acrimonious dialogue with officials, no rubbishing of opponents, no unfair tactics. He was the sort of champion who would be a credit to any sport.

Coached by his father, a Melbourne businessman, Hunt came to the fore early on, winning the Victorian Junior Championship at the age of fifteen. The following year, he took the Victorian Championship itself and won it every year until 1971. Barrington got his first glimpse of this prodigy in 1965 when the seventeen-year old Australian arrived in London with Dick Carter and Ken Hiscoe to take part in the British Amateur. Hunt was bronzed, fit and precociously talented. He reached the final and, although he lost to Jawaid, he was by no means disgraced. He was clearly a coming man.

The two players from whom he learned most were Ken Hiscoe and Jonah Barrington. Hiscoe, almost ten years older, had started out as a lifeguard on a beach and there was something of the exploding surf in his play. Bold, spectacular and fiercely competitive, he hit the ball with destructive force. Hunt was to emulate his use of the volley and to learn many other things from his compatriot. It was fitting that they turned professional together in 1971. ·

Barrington was a late starter. While Hunt was contesting his first British Amateur, his future rival was still toiling at his lowly desk job with the SRA and struggling so much with his game that he could not even make the Hampstead Cricket Club Cumberland Cup squash team. When the two players met in Australia the following season, Hunt inflicted a humiliating defeat. The senior man by six years, Barrington was made to feel like a floundering novice. Only a year later, however, he had won the British Open and the British Amateur to become the unofficial world champion.

Having overhauled Hunt, Barrington stayed there by virtue of his superior fitness and self-discipline. His game was shorn of all extravagance. He depended on safe, accurate length shots and trained assiduously to make sure that he could move around a squash court faster and longer than anyone else. Nobody had attempted this kind of physical conditioning before or seen the need for it. After all, it was only an amateur sport. Barrington led the way with dedicated professionalism.

Nasrullah Khan believed in holding on to an advantage. His players were there to win, not to help others perform more effectively against them. 'Never tell them anything,' he would say. Barrington did not heed this advice. In the fifth game of the Australian Open final in 1970, he noticed that Hunt was suffering so badly from cramp that he was receiving service by standing on one leg. Barrington was an easy winner against an opponent with such a handicap. He also observed that, while he was sweating profusely, Hunt simply turned a ghastly white.

When Barrington described the condition to a physiotherapist, he was told it was probably caused by a lack of sodium. The advice was duly passed on to Hunt who started to take slow-release sodium tablets that cured his problems. This was an indication of what Naz saw as a weakness in his player – a willingness to assist others. In yielding to such impulses, Barrington would in time become the architect of his own eclipse. He held nothing back. A fanatical squash evangelist, he was always preaching the gospel and telling of his own conversion on the road to the Lansdowne Club. In discussing his training methods so openly and in stressing the importance of the right mental approach, he gave his opponents ammunition which could be used against him.

Once Hunt followed suit and drove himself to peak fitness, he dispatched Barrington, then put distance between them. His game had more variety, his shots were more penetrating, his killer instinct was sharper, his powers of recovery were even more phenomenal and his imagination on court was far greater. Coolness itself, Hunt never allowed any doubts to trouble him and he kept his emotions under stern control.

This was the sovereign of the new order, the man whom the Pakistanis had to chase. Leading the pack were four players of consummate ability – Qamar Zaman, Gogi Alauddin, Hiddy Jahan and Mohibullah Khan, who, though born in Peshawar, was not part of the Khan dynasty and who is often referred to as Mohibullah junior to distinguish him from his namesake. Three of these players were Pathans. Two of them – Zaman and Mohibullah – were coached at the Peshawar training centre by Umar Daraz Khan who had become related to the dynasty when he married Safirullah's daughter.

After showing a preference for tennis, Qamar Zaman concentrated on squash at fifteen. He was to become one of the game's finest creative artists, an undisciplined genius who was never less than entertaining and who was often more than merely brilliant. Shortish, slight and with the mobile features of a natural clown, Zaman's totally unorthodox approach was like a breath of fresh air in a sport where too many players settled for the safety and monotony of long rallies.

Gogi Alauddin from Lahore was the Asian equivalent of one of L. S. Lowry's matchstick men. Weighing less than nine stone and with a twenty-eight inch waist, he was a distinctive figure on court, where he could bring much bigger men crashing down with a lethal combination of agility, concentration, anticipation and unnerving ball control. Shy and serene by nature, he seemed to float through a game like an apparition, haunting his opponents until they took fright and gave in.

Hiddy Jahan was also born in Lahore but his family moved when he was a boy and settled in Quetta. Coached by his father, Mumtaz Khan, and by Gulam Hussain, another local professional, Hiddy later went down to Lahore where he became a close friend of Alauddin. The tall, sturdy, powerful Pathan made the little Punjabi look even more like a stick insect in squash gear but games between them were events of wonder. With instinctive timing, Hiddy learned to hit the ball as hard as anyone in the sport. To watch him play is to see two major historical components of the game blended into one – the hearty brutality of the British public school and the subtle alchemy of the Pathan tradition.

When Alauddin, Jahan and another friend, Sajjad Muneer, went to England in 1970 under the auspices of the Punjab Sports Control Board, they all distinguished themselves in their first British Amateur Championship. Jahan reached the quarter finals, where he lost to Alauddin, Muneer got to the semi-finals, and Alauddin himself won the event at the first attempt, returning the next year to take the title again. They were hungry for success and spurred on by memories of what the Khans had achieved for their young country.

Mohibullah Khan junior was one of eleven children born to a poor family. Unlike Zaman, Jahan and Alauddin, whose fathers were all squash professionals, he had no automatic link with the sport. Until 1968 he was a 'tennis boy' at the PAF Officers' Club in Peshawar where Hashim Khan had his first coaching job. Mohibullah's natural flair for squash gained him entry to the training centre which had been built in 1967 by the far-sighted Nur Khan to develop the latent talents of the local youth. The new recruit worked hard and his all-round game prospered.

When he entered international competition for the first time in 1971, it was with startling success. Still only fifteen, he won the British Junior Championship and competed in the World Junior. He was seventeen when he won the British Amateur in 1973, beating Zaman in the final. The next year, he was still only a teenager when he won the Australian Open Championship without conceding a single game, collecting the scalps of Jahan, Hunt and Hiscoe in the last three matches. The stringy player with the straggly moustache and the piping voice was making everyone sit up and take notice.

Aman, Rahmat and Torsam were also in hot pursuit of Hunt

so Pakistan had enviable strength in depth. The Khans were not yet ready to operate as full-time professionals, however. When Town and Country Clubs opened its new Squash Leicester centre, Nasrullah was appointed as advisor with Torsam as coach. Rahmat was at a sister club in Welling, Kent before moving to Newham. He was offered the chance to go to Paris to coach at the group's Montparnasse club but he declined and sent Hiddy Jahan's brother in his place. Rahmat often met Torsam in Leicester which had a thriving squash community. The Khans flourished there as coaches. Meanwhile, their reputations as players were growing.

In April 1974, Torsam won the Harp Lager National Tournament which was held at Croydon. His opponent was Mike Thurger, an English international who had been the beaten finalist three times in the event already. Torsam showed no sympathy for him. After letting the first game slip away from him, he began to hit a perfect length and turned on the pressure to wrap up the match in forty-five minutes. The score was 3–1. A couple of press reports compared Torsam's style with that of Roshan Khan. Like his father, he played some amazing strokes, killing the ball particularly well on the backhand and executing the most deft drop shots. Thurger, coincidentally, was a master at Millfield, the school where Sharif Khan had been educated.

Torsam continued to play well and was unbeaten when he came up against his cousin in the final of the Mercia Men's Tournament in Stourbridge. He was in magnificent form again, conceding only five points and winning 9–1, 9–1, 9–3. Some scintillating squash was played and both men contributed towards an intriguing evening. The tournament was held early in November. Later that month, Torsam stormed on to achieve a convincing win in the final of the Welsh Open, defeating Kaoud 9–2, 9–0, 9–2. He had the additional satisfaction of avenging Rahmat's elimination in the semi-final by the Egyptian player.

A couple of days later, Torsam was back in action again. The occasion was the opening of the championship court at the new Wembley Squash Centre. Unveiling a commemorative plaque, the Duke of Edinburgh, patron of the Squash Rackets Association, pointed out that 'the real value of this championship court is that with spectators and television coverage, it will bring the game to a very much wider audience'. To mark the event, a team from the SRA took on a side drawn from the International Squash Players Association.

As befitted a man who helped to create ISPA, Jonah Barrington was chosen to lead the professional team. Their 6–2 win secured them the Dunlop Trophy. Barrington himself launched the evening with a shortened version of a coaching clinic. His humorous anecdotes about Nasrullah Khan had the audience roaring with laughter but there was a fund of good will behind the amusement. Naz was much loved and he was respected by all as the best coach in the business.

Honoured to be selected for the ISPA team, Torsam played some flowing squash in the first match to beat the more experienced Mike Corby. The quality of his play demonstrated just how much he had improved since moving to Britain, the squash capital of the world. Torsam's performance that evening, however, was overshadowed by Ahmed Safwat who turned in a dazzling display to trounce Peter Verow. Highlights of the occasion were later shown by BBC Television. It was the shape of things to come.

1975 was to be a good year for Pakistani players in general and for Torsam in particular. At the Slazenger Chichester Open in January, he got to the semi-final before losing in a thriller to Safwat. It was one of the finest matches of the season. Torsam raced into a 2–0 lead, Safwat fought back to square the match, then the two of them put on a grandstand finish which was eventually decided 10–8 in the Egyptian's favour.

The same month, the same two players had survived a qualifying competition to take part in a new, prestigious, round-robin event. It was a five-leg grand prix circuit that was sponsored by British Caledonian Airways and Yellow Dot Sportswear. The event was spread over three months, each leg comprising three days' play. Total prize money exceeding £21,000 was at stake. The most that any individual could earn was £3500 and the least was £600. To squash players of the day it was good money for fifteen days' work.

The world's eight leading professionals had been chosen for

the event – Geoff Hunt, Jonah Barrington, Ken Hiscoe, Cam Nancarrow, Gogi Alauddin, Hiddy Jahan, Ahmed Safwat and Torsam Khan: three Australians, three Pakistanis, one Briton and one Egyptian. It was a fair reflection of the wider squash scene. The notable absentee was Qamar Zaman who was not eligible as he had not yet turned professional.

Torsam was in august company and determined to make the most of his opportunity, especially as the first leg was being held in Leicester where he was still based. Subsequent venues were Edinburgh, Manchester, Newcastle and Wembley. Torsam was thrown in at the deep end, drawing the reigning world champion in the first match. He fought hard but Hunt was too strong and too resourceful for him. Barrington had to scratch from the first round because his wife – he and Madeline had married in 1973 – was expecting a baby.

The British player must have wished he had missed the second night as well because it was not a happy occasion for him. Torsam Khan beat him 3–1 to spring the first shock of the leg. The manner of his victory brought him criticism, however. Eagerness led to outright aggression and Barrington had to withstand some very provocative behaviour. At the end of the match, the loser did not pause to offer the ritual handshake but simply walked off court in disgust. Torsam nevertheless had beaten the legendary player and it was something to savour.

There was more bad blood next day when Torsam came face to face with Ken Hiscoe. Competitive tensions boiled over and the match descended into a disputatious muddle. Torsam came off worst for his opponent was not a man to be intimidated by hostile glares and robust tactics. Hiscoe was bigger, stronger and much more experienced. Also, he had the crowd on his side. Torsam's antics led to his being barracked and his constant appeal for lets did not help his cause. Hiscoe ran out the winner, leaving his opponent in sixth place after the first leg of the circuit. Of Torsam's ability, there was no doubt. He was bursting with it. His temperament was what let him down.

The Benson and Hedges British Open now loomed. It was to be Pakistan's year. Torsam and Rahmat sailed through the first round but the latter perished in the second. The younger cousin kept his hopes alive with another victory but it was as far as he would go. In the third round, he took on Cam Nancarrow in an ill-tempered game that kept the officials very busy. The big Australian eventually won 3–2 but not before Torsam had pushed his awkward opponent to the limit. The round was also to see Barrington, wreak his revenge on the mournful Mo Yasin.

Zaman disposed of Geoff Hunt in the quarter finals. There would be a new Open champion. Barrington, Nancarrow and Mohibullah Khan were also ousted. The semi-finals paired Zaman with Jahan, and Alauddin with Hiscoe. Three Pakistanis and one Australian. There was thus a strong possibility that the title would go East, and so it proved. After weaving enough magic to defeat Jahan in the semi-final, Qamar Zaman went on to beat Alauddin in straight games. Though he was born in Quetta, Zaman's family came from Peshawar. After a thirteen-year gap, the title returned to Khan country once more.

Torsam continued to participate in the grand prix circuit as it moved on to its second leg in Edinburgh. Hiddy Jahan destroyed him in his first outing. Off court, however, they remained great friends. The event had its lighter side as Jahan fondly remembers: 'The Yellow Dot series was fun. During the games, most of the boys sat up in the gallery and watched. We used to put money in a kitty, then bet on how many lets there'd be in a match. Whoever got closest won the money. It was usually twenty or thirty quid. Sometimes more. When Torsam played, the bidding would start around a hundred. He was always appealing for a let. Certain players brought out the worst in him. He always had trouble with Nancarrow and Hiscoe. In a match with them, there might be two hundred appeals for a let.'

Torsam was a popular member of the octet when they were socialising. He treated the whole series as a learning experience. Tossed in among the best players in the world, he took time to adjust and to curb his temper. Though he finished near the bottom at the end of the day, it did not matter. He had earned the right to consort with the top players and he had been accepted by them.

Early in April of that year, ISPA published its ranking list of the top sixteen. It made interesting reading.

1.	Qamar Zaman	(Pakistan)
2.	Geoff Hunt	(Australia)
3.	Gogi Alauddin	(Pakistan)
4.	Hiddy Jahan	(Pakistan)
5.	Mohibullah Khan	(Pakistan)
6.	Ken Hiscoe	(Australia)
7.	Jonah Barrington	(Britain)
8.	Cam Nancarrow	(Australia)
9.	Ahmed Safwat	(Egypt)
10.	Torsam Khan	(Pakistan)
11.	Roland Watson	(South Africa)
12.	Sajjad Muneer	(Pakistan)
13.	Rahmat Khan	(Pakistan)
14.	Bill Reedman	(Australia)
15.	Mo Yasin	(Pakistan)
16.	John Easter	(Britain)

Four Pakistanis were in the top five and another four in the top sixteen. Most of them were relatively young, still developing, not yet at their peak. It was a worrying situation for the other nationalities. Australia had only half the firepower of its main rivals. Time was not on its side. Hunt and Nancarrow were in their late twenties and Hiscoe was well into his thirties. Jonah Barrington waved the British flag alone in the top ten. He was supported on the fringe of the rankings by John Easter, an amiable giant who had once represented Oxford University at both squash and cricket, and who would probably have climbed much higher as a professional but for the fitness problems associated with his bulk.

Rahmat and Torsam continued to justify their positions in the rankings and to hold out hopes of another world champion for the dynasty. Both performed well on the circuit without getting really close to any of the major titles. Rahmat's game had the sustained brilliance that was the Khan hallmark but he lacked a knockout punch. Having rocked his opponents and got them on the ropes, he usually gave them time to clear their heads and come out punching. Again, he had some unfortunate injuries along the way. Notwithstanding all this, he was an

outstanding touch player who could take games off the likes of
Hunt, Zaman and Alauddin.

Torsam had enough innate ability to go right to the top.
Stamina and temperament were his weaknesses. Hiddy Jahan
used to urge him to train properly if he wanted the number one
spot. A Torsam Khan who was still firing on all cylinders in the
fifth game would be a fearsome opponent. But he was unable
to take on the kind of punitive training schedules that had
transformed Barrington and Hunt into world-beaters. Unknown
to anyone else, Torsam was already forcing himself through
personal pain barriers and subjecting himself to the kinds of
pressures that would in time claim his life.

Naz, Rahmat and Aman also persuaded him of the folly of
losing his temper on court. Their reasoning was sound.
Confrontational squash was self-defeating. It upset officials
and spectators alike. It was bad for the image of a game they
were there to promote. Torsam accepted all the criticism that
was levelled against him. When the new season began, he
made a special effort to curb his headstrong behaviour and to
devote all his energies to playing the game instead of arguing
about it. There was a visible improvement and everyone –
including Torsam himself – was pleased. The young lion was
his own tamer. It augured well for the future.

Unfortunately, he had a relapse at the worst possible time.
When the Lucas British Open and World Championships were
held at Wembley in February 1976, Torsam lost his cool once
more. In the third round he came up against his old adversary,
Ken Hiscoe. It was eyeball-to-eyeball time. The match was
bedevilled by aggravation from start to finish. It took no
account of the fact that squash is a non-contact sport. The fiery
Pakistani and the rugged Australian pushed, prodded and
pummelled each other throughout four frenetic games. No
fewer than eighty-four lets were awarded and there were
twelve other refereeing decisions. Mike Palmer, then of the
Daily Express, wrote an impassioned article about the damage
such behaviour could do to the sport. He blamed both players
and summed up their battle in the perfect phrase – 'a crunch
match'.

Immediately afterwards, the players were unrepentant.

Hiscoe pointed out that they always had that type of match. Because they both hit a lot of shots that finished up in the centre of the court, there was bound to be physical contact. Torsam agreed with this assessment. He argued that the crowd did not know the rules and said that all his appeals for lets were justified. When he had calmed down a little, he admitted that he had allowed himself to get riled.

The tragedy was that both men played some delightful squash. In amongst the barging and the buffeting were some absolute gems. Hiscoe volleyed superbly and Torsam put his full range of shots on display. There were vintage rallies but they were marred by all the nonsense going on around them. The other sad fact was that Torsam had a genuine chance to win and cause an upset. By reverting to his old self, he squandered an opportunity that he should have taken.

Press response was uniform. The two players were condemned for taking the name of the game too literally and attempting to squash the fight out of each other. Many other complaints were passed on verbally to the players. Torsam responded well. When he took part in the Durham Open later in the month, his self-control was above reproach. He remained even-tempered in the face of some real provocation on court from Mo Yasin with whom he was not the best of friends. He was schooling himself to behave with more restraint so that a fiasco like the Hiscoe match did not occur again.

Outside his tournament commitments, he still had to earn his living. The squash club in Leicester got into financial hot water and went bust. Torsam returned for a while to his old job in Wimbledon and Rahmat went across to Wembley. Nasrullah was still coaching at Edgbaston Priory and Aman was also in Birmingham, at the courts attached to the Albany Hotel. The three younger Khans advanced on two fronts, consolidating their reputations as coaches and inching their way up the rankings as players.

April gave them a welcome reason to return to Pakistan. Squash enthusiasts were offered a double treat. Pakistan International Airlines, the game's generous sponsors in that country, combined an Open Championship with a World Team Tournament. The two events were held together to celebrate the opening of the new PIA Squash Complex, one of the finest purpose-built centres of its kind. The magnificent championship court seated over two hundred and fifty with standing room for an additional hundred. Like the Peshawar Centre, the complex was the brainchild of Retired Air Marshall Nur Khan, one of the most powerful men in the country and a loyal friend to the game of squash.

Since the Team Tournament revolved around the Hashim Khan Trophy, the great man was tempted back to Karachi from the lusher pastures of Denver, Colorado, where he now worked. Khans abounded. Indeed, it was less like a tournament than a tribal gathering.

Mohibullah senior came over with his brother, Gul Ahmed, and another America-based Pakistani professional, to represent their new country. As resident coach at the Sind Club, their father, Safirullah, was on the spot already. Two of Hashim's sons, Sharif and Aziz, flew in to compete. Azam Khan came from London to watch. Roshan Khan was still living in Karachi where he coached, among others, Karimullah Khan, who had the distinction of being Torsam's uncle even though he was three years younger than him. Torsam himself was there with Rahmat and Aman. Jahangir was given the honour of carrying the rackets for the Pakistan Professionals Team. Dozens of other relatives converged on the tournament.

Squash runs in the Khan family – at high speed. In other Pathan households, it moves at a more sedate pace. Mohamed Amin, guileful coach at the Gymkhana Club, proudly accompanied his three sons – Mo Yasin, Mohamed Saleem and Maqsood Ahmed – who were all taking part. Mohibullah junior was playing alongside his brother, Atlas Khan, while another brother, seven-year old Jansher, stayed at home in Peshawar and dreamed of the time when his chance would come. The Gul brothers were competing, Qamar Zaman was there with his brother, and yet another family double-act would have been on the bill if Shah Jahan had been joined by his younger but more illustrious brother, Hiddy. The latter was in temporary exile because he had flouted Sports Board policy by competing in South Africa. Happily, the suspension was lifted after the PIA tournament.

With prize money of over £10,000, the Open Championship was the richest in the game and this was mirrored in the strength of the field. The cream of the squash world had poured in. Apart from Jahan, only Roland Watson, Bill Reedman, John Easter and Ken Hiscoe were missing, and the last two had been scheduled to appear. Easter was scratched when he, unaccountably, failed to turn up in time for the team event and Hiscoe had to withdraw at the last moment to fly home to Sydney where his wife had been taken ill. This still left sixty-four players keyed up for action. Standards and tensions were high.

In terms of the future development of the game, the World Team Tournament carried more significance but it refused to catch fire. Visiting teams were muted, jet-lagged or – as in the cases of Britain and Australia – hopelessly weakened by the absence of crucial players. The home teams romped through to the final. Satisfying as this was for the local support, it did rob the event of any real import and drama. In the final, the Professional trio of Zaman, Alauddin and Mohibullah junior beat the Pakistan Amateurs – Mohamed Saleem, Atlas Khan and Maqsood Ahmed – by an emphatic 3–0 margin. One of the few pairings to savour was the clash of the two Mohibullahs when the United States took on the eventual winners.

Hashim Khan presented the trophy that bore his name and then turned his attention to the individual event, anxious for his first glimpse at Geoff Hunt. At Wembley in February, Hunt had become both British Open Champion and World Open champion. Hashim was duly impressed: 'He play good game. Very smart. Good reflexes. Always ready to hit. He stop ball and he finish ball.'

Geoff Hunt was not pleased with the conditions. There was no air conditioning and temperatures were almost sub-tropical. The heat made the ball bouncy and difficult to put away. Barrington came up against the worst humidity he ever encountered during his semi-final against Mohibullah junior. The sweltering heat reduced him to a grease spot and Mohibullah – aided by the presence of President Bhutto – put the British player out of the event in short order.

The Khan challenge faded early on and the top seeds

contested the closing stages. Mastering the conditions much better, Gogi Alauddin beat Hunt in the final.

Seven world champions lined up for a historic photograph outside the complex: Hashim, Azam, Roshan, Mohibullah, Hunt, Barrington and Zaman. The Khans relived their moments of glory in front of the camera. They were bound to succumb to nostalgia. They looked back with fond eyes and light hearts to the years of their dominance. There had been fewer players then and levels of fitness were not perhaps as high, but their achievements still gave them prime positions in the hall of fame. Nobody in the PIA tournament had shown Hashim's smiling authority, Azam's darting brilliance, Roshan's effortless precision or Mohibullah senior's frantic commitment.

Who would take over from them? Who would restore family pride? In a clan as large and talented as theirs, there had to be someone who could become world champion. The laws of genetic inheritance dictated it. Tradition compelled it. They expected it.

Who would fulfil the dynastic ambition? Unknown to them, he was already lurking in the shadows. But there were two drawbacks. He was only twelve years old. And he had been forbidden to play squash.

JAHANGIR

Jahangir Khan was born in Karachi on 10 December 1963. He was a sickly child, the youngest, smallest and weakest in the family. In every sense, he was at the end of the queue. The doctor diagnosed a double hernia. Operations would be necessary when the boy was older. In the meantime, he was to be kept away from anything strenuous as it would aggravate his condition. It was a dreadful sentence to pass on a male child. His most natural instincts were stifled. Brought up in the narrow back-streets of Abyssinia Lines, he had the mortification of watching other children run and jump and play and fight and do all the other things that he was not permitted to do. His elder brothers, Torsam and Hassan, were fit and healthy. Why was he so different?

At the age of five, he had his first operation. He came from a poor family and grew up with only the necessities of life around him. But he had one thing in his favour: his father, Roshan, was the squash professional at the Fleet Club. Technically, he served in the Navy so Jahangir was able to receive medical treatment at the Naval Hospital. Most families in Karachi would not have been able to afford the operation. When their children are born with double hernias or worse afflictions, they have to learn to live with them. Among the beggar gangs of the city, some hideous disabilities and deformities go on show every day.

Roshan's profession gave Jahangir another advantage. It allowed the boy a fantasy world into which he could escape. His father had been world squash champion. Jahangir fantasized about what it would be like to occupy such an exalted position. Because of the physical limitations of his own life, the more cherished and detailed became his fantasy existence. Squash was a daily topic of conversation at the little house. Names of the great were bandied about so frequently that Jahangir felt he knew them all personally. On the squash court of his mind, he regularly beat Jonah Barrington, outfoxed Qamar Zaman and exhausted Geoff Hunt in a war of attrition.

The boy was eight when Roshan gave him his first racket with the shaft cut-down. It was a gesture more than anything else, a toy, a distraction, a plaything to keep him occupied. Roshan did not think for a moment that it might be the tool with which his son might one day make his living. Jahangir was still the delicate child who had to be protected from his own exuberance. Torsam and Hassan were the squash players. Their younger brother could just have fun wielding his own racket.

Jahangir took a different view. Possession of the treasured racket served to fuel his fantasies. He learned how to hold it properly and how to execute the basic strokes of the game. It never seemed to be out of his hand. Far from being a toy, it became an organic part of him, an additional limb with a swishing life of its own. He bombarded his father and his brothers with questions about the game. His enthusiasm knew no bounds. He had a surging determination to carry on the family tradition.

At the age of ten, he was taken along to the Fleet Club but his father would only allow him to have a hit once a week. It was deeply frustrating. Respect for his father made him obey at first but the lure of the game became too strong. He *had* to prove himself on a squash court. He was a Khan. They were denying him his birthright. Jahangir therefore began to practise in secret. During siesta time, and again at dusk, he would sneak off to the deserted Fleet Club and play on his own. In the heat of the midday sun, he would become one long dribble of sweat but he never gave up.

Jahangir has vivid memories of these early days: 'I was so keen on squash that I wanted to play at a very early age. But doctor didn't allow me to play because I had a hernia problem, and doctor said to my father that he won't be able to play all his life. But I was very keen on the game and not listen. And I used

99

to play all day in the hot weather. I mean, nobody can play in that heat. Everyone was resting in the room or sleeping inside. I used to play outside, sweating too much.'

Roshan did not know whether to scold him or praise him when he found out what had been going on. After all, he, Nasrullah and their other brothers used to practise on the British Army courts when their own father was not about. It was well worth the occasional beating from Faizullah if they were found out. Roshan did not suspect Jahangir. He did not think the boy was strong enough to play squash in such humidity: 'He always used to watch me, and ask how you play squash. "Daddy, how you hit this stroke, how you hold the racket?" This sort of question he was asking, and I was answering. When he came home from school, he used to say "Okay, Daddy, I'm going to sleep in the room." Then he took his racket and cycled to the squash club.'

By the age of twelve, he was ready for a second operation. It was successful. As soon as he had convalesced, he went back to his private training routine, practising his ball control, learning to hit harder, slowly building up his strength. His natural aptitude for the game meant that he improved by leaps and bounds. Roshan was persuaded that perhaps he might be a squash player after all. There were no adverse effects after the operation. Jahangir was filling out and his legs were quite sturdy. His father began to coach him in earnest. With professional guidance of that calibre, his true worth soon emerged.

But he was still not seen as a future champion. There was a long way to go yet. He had to take his turn in the queue. It was Torsam who still bore the family hopes. He had earned his place in the top ten and he was good enough to hold it. Eleven years older than Jahangir, he was idolised by his younger brother. There was a swashbuckling quality about Torsam that was very endearing. He had verve and dash. When he was at home, the house was always filled with fun and laughter. Jahangir was sad when his brother went away and he used to wait patiently for letters and press cuttings and photographs. Torsam was his role model. He had shown that there was a way out of the poverty and the limited horizons of Karachi.

Indeed, for boys like them it was virtually the only way out. A squash racket was their exit visa.

Jahangir still luxuriated in his fantasies but he was realistic enough to know that it might be a very long time before they became true. Khan champions took years to mature. Hashim had been thirty-five when he won his first world title. In fact, according to A. J. Quraishi, former Secretary of the Pakistan SRA, he may have been born as early as 1914, making him thirty-seven when he stooped to conquer. At all events, he was definitely past forty when he bagged his last title. Roshan had been thirty, Azam thirty-three. Mohibullah senior was only twenty-four when he hit the jackpot but he was the exception that proved the rule.

The Khans were slow starters. Reflecting on it all in 1976, Jahangir saw that he might have to wait fifteen, even twenty years before he climbed to the summit of the game. It was a chilling prospect but he was not discouraged. His early experiences in life had taught him to be very patient. He had none of Torsam's impetuosity. He was ready to get his head down and put in the hard graft. His determination and willingness to train hard was astounding in one so young. He was an apt pupil and a gift to any coach.

Though he still dreamed of being world champion, Jahangir was convinced that he would have to stay in line behind his brother. Torsam would get there in time and become the first world champion from the Khan dynasty who had actually been born in Pakistan. His predecessors had all grown up in British India. There was more at stake now for the new country needed all the kudos it could get. Success on the squash court was thus a political act. That was why the President took the trouble to visit the PIA Complex during its inaugural tournament. Winning a world title would not just boost family pride, it would confer social status on the new champion and guarantee his financial security.

After suffering dreadful birth pangs, the new country was not given a decent interval to recover. Internal and external troubles assaulted it. After eleven years of corrupt and inefficient 'democratic' government, General Ayub Khan set up the first military government in 1958. There were agrarian and industrial reforms during his rule but they did not assuage the burgeoning resentment. In 1969, he was succeeded by General Yahya Khan who was woefully ineffectual. Discontent rumbled in East Pakistan where the standard of living was lower, the representation in government was smaller, and the share of overseas aid and development projects was disproportionately tiny.

Two events split the country in 1970. A murderous cyclone brought East Pakistan to its knees, and its western half was mean and slow in giving assistance. Then, in December 1970, an election was held to return the country to civil authority. A one-person, one-vote franchise was instituted. Calamity ensued. In East Pakistan, the Awami League, led by Mujibur Rahman, won all but two of the seats. The Pakistan People's Party, headed by Zulfikar Ali Bhutto, was the dominant party in the western sector, taking a little over half of the seats. Which party should rule? The question provoked a constitutional crisis. As a result, Mujibur Rahman was arrested and thrown into gaol.

This sparked off an insurrection in East Pakistan and the army moved in. Such was its cruelty that it prompted bitter guerilla opposition. Flooded with Bengali refugees, India finally stepped in and declared war on its neighbour. The Pakistan army was defeated in the east and Bangladesh came into being. West Pakistan was now simply Pakistan.

Its affairs were far from settled. Bhutto came to power and governed until 1977 when he was ousted in a bloodless coup d'état over his re-election. Loud protests arose over his apparent rigging of the votes. The main issue of the day was whether or not there should be a re-run of the election. As a year or more passed, Pakistan drifted closer and closer to civil war.

Jahangir Khan was thus living in troubled times. When Bhutto was deposed, the boy was still only thirteen. His squash had improved, his commitment had deepened and he had clarified his ambitions. He was just one of many young hopefuls on the junior squash scene and he had resigned himself to an interminable wait. He was not to know that the man who eventually succeeded Bhutto – Prime Minister Junejo – would one day meet him at Downing Street where they were both guests of the British Prime Minister. What kept Jahangir going at such a furious pace was not the thought of being feted as a celebrity, it was his unwavering belief in the three abstracts that Pakistan used as its national motto: Unity. Faith. Discipline.

Unity was the basis of his family life. He was part of a close-knit group that offered unfailing support. From his Muslim faith, he was to draw tremendous strength. Discipline came from within. He had learned it during the lost years of his early childhood when he had to hold back, and during his clandestine sessions at the Fleet Club. Jahangir was a quiet, serious, withdrawn boy. As the last in the family, he was at the bottom of the pecking order. It influenced his character: he was watchful, attentive, unobtrusive. He could laugh with the rest of them when Torsam was at home but he had an old head on young shoulders. He was prepared to take on responsibilities that would have frightened most children of his age.

Hassan was his immediate senior. He was a taciturn youth, slow, unhurried and rather somnolent. He, too, was a promising squash player but Jahangir soon overhauled him. Hassan reached county standard but could not progress much further. He was thus in the unfortunate position of being nutcrackered by the two most shining talents in the family. To his credit, he took on his role without complaint and was never less than willing to be a practise partner for Torsam and Jahangir. If they succeeded, he would be delighted to share in the glory.

Squash now monopolised Jahangir's existence. He was still at school but had to struggle to keep his mind on his work. No matter how hard his father pushed him, he was always ready for more. The weak child with a double hernia had become a wiry youth with ever-growing reserves of stamina. Roshan had learned from the mistake that he and Nasrullah had made. Both of them smoked heavily and neglected to train as vigorously as they should have done. Each paid the penalty. It would not happen to Jahangir. He would have deficiencies but they would not be in the area of fitness.

News filtered back regularly from Britain and Jahangir was more anxious than ever to hear it. There was now a real chance that he might one day join his brother and cousins abroad. Torsam was playing well on the circuit, maintaining his position in the rankings without quite being able to make a decisive thrust upwards. Rahmat, too, was still dazzling spectators with his skills and he moved up to twelfth position. Tournaments were taking them far afield. Post cards would arrive at the Karachi home from Australia, New Zealand, Canada, the Far East and all parts of Europe.

In the summer of 1977 the bombshell was dropped. News arrived of the sudden death of Nasrullah Khan. He had died of a heart attack at the age of fifty-seven. Nobody could believe it. Naz had always seemed so fit and alert. He had just embarked on a new venture in Stoke-on-Trent where he had gone into partnership with the former England goalkeeper, Gordon Banks. Everyone was shattered. Naz had been such a powerful presence in their lives that it was hard to envisage how they could cope without him.

His funeral was held at a Birmingham mosque and attended by many friends from Britain as well as by members of his own family. His sphere of influence had been wide and lasting. If anyone was coached by Naz, even for just an hour or two, it was an experience that they would never forget. He had a knack of explaining and enlarging the game. He did not simply make his pupils grind away at repetitive exercises. He talked to them about the philosophy of the game. With the gentlemanly Nasrullah Khan as their guide, they were taken for a stroll through an enchanted garden full of wondrous sights and scents. He showed that there was much more to squash than the smell of sweat.

Jonah Barrington was at the funeral. When Aman had rung him to break the sad news, he had been devastated. Coach and player had been through so much together. Barrington regretted that they had not been able to resolve their differences in recent years. Naz had been a surrogate father to him and he wept like a bereaved son. Though his career had moved on dramatically since those early days with Naz at the Lansdowne Club, he freely acknowledged the debt he owed to the coach. Barrington felt privileged when he was asked to be a senior at the funeral.

Roshan was stunned by it all. He had relied on his elder

brother for so many years now and profited from his coaching and advice. Even though Naz lived thousands of miles away, they had remained close in spirit. Rahmat, Aman and Torsam were consumed with grief. Naz had been a salient feature of the squash scene in Britain for a quarter of a century. The domed forehead, the laughing eyes, the pencil moustache above a broad grin and the gracious manner would all be missed. So, too, would his habit of grabbing you by the shoulders when he had criticism to impart. Nasrullah Khan was unique. A great value passed out of all their lives.

But his influence continued: Roshan coached his younger son by tapping his vast reservoir of knowledge about the game, much of it gained from Nasrullah. He did not try to mould Jahangir into a version of himself – exciting strokeplay was a vital ingredient of squash but it was not enough on its own. The game had to be played with the head as well as the heart. Look at Geoff Hunt for example: the world champion had trained himself out of any flashy shots. His stamina was so exceptional that opponents knew they had to keep him on court for at least two hours in order to beat him, which gave him an immense psychological advantage.

Jahangir was encouraged to adopt the same approach, to build his stamina, play a tight game, frustrate his adversaries and force them into errors. By the time he was fourteen, he had made such progress that Roshan was amazed. The doctor must have been dumbfounded. According to medical science, what was happening was impossible. Jahangir was supposed to avoid vigorous exercise yet here he was excelling himself at one of the most taxing of sports. He was also part of a junior colts coaching scheme so he had a back-up to his father's help. He was a tall, slender, long-faced youth with a strong right arm and a wrist of steel. He had powerful lungs and legs, sharp reflexes, good concentration, an even temperament and an indomitable spirit.

It was time to put him to the test. In November 1978, when he was still only fourteen, he competed in the National Juniors' Individual Squash Championship. The event was held on the courts at the PAF Squash Centre in Peshawar. Even after Partition, the link between sport and the military was retained.

There could not be a more appropriate place for the young Pathan to set out his wares. He was going home.

In front of a packed audience, Jahangir took on the title-holder Ramshaid Gul. He played percentage squash, risking nothing, containing his opponent, retrieving every shot like a frisky spaniel. When he was two games in the lead, he became over-confident and went for his shots. It was an unwise change of tactics. Gul got back in the match and took the third game. Reverting to his technique of wearing down his man, Jahangir took control in the fourth and won the match 3–1. New hopes soared. He was national champion.

Two months later, he caused a major upset in the National Open Squash Rackets Championship at the PIA Complex in Karachi. Over five long and gruelling games, he got the better of top-seeded Mohamed Saleem, a much older and more experienced player. Even a cut over the left eyebrow in the fifth game did not deter Jahangir. Injury slowed him down in the quarter-finals where he lost to Saleem's brother, Maqsood Ahmed, but he had served notice that he would be a handful for anyone in the future. At that stage he was still a student in the ninth class at the Government Model Secondary School PECHS.

When PIA sent a team of its top amateurs on a tour of South-East Asia, Jahangir was invited along with two other juniors to get some experience of international competition. He acquitted himself well and was later selected for a Pakistan Junior Team which played in Sweden. When his commitments in Scandinavia were over, he flew to London to visit his brother.

Torsam was delighted to see him and asked if he would like to stay. The boy was thrilled. Karachi was not the ideal place to train. Its climate could be oppressive on a squash court and there were very few tournaments available for young players. Britain was the perfect place to hone his skills. After living in a country which had relatively few courts, Jahangir was in one that had thousands. Moreover, he would be with his big brother which was a treat in itself.

Rahmat and Aman were very pleased to see him and offered to help all they could. Jahangir was introduced to Rahmat's attractive young wife, Josephine, who had been a receptionist at the Wembley Squash Centre. The newly-weds had a flat in Wembley that the boy would get to know very well indeed in time. Rahmat had also become a businessman. Looking ahead and beyond his playing days, he and two partners had taken the enterprising move of setting up a company to produce squash rackets. Their trade name was Unsquashable. It made people laugh but they remembered it.

Torsam's own flat was in Sutton, Surrey. Because Jahangir's spoken English was still rather weak, his brother arranged for him to have lessons for a couple of hours every day at a private language school in Streatham. Joyce Wadey was a friend who lived nearby and worked for ILEA in Lambeth. She volunteered to drive Jahangir to the school every morning on her way to work: 'He was a delightful boy. Jahangir couldn't speak much English at first but he soon improved. We used to talk about squash – I played myself at the Wimbledon Club, which was how I got to know Torsam. Jahangir always made some comment about our weather which was a bit different from Pakistan. Oh, yes, then there was my driving. That was always good for a joke.'

Hassan came to visit for a short while as well. He brought another relative, Zair Khan. The three boys had a lot of fun with Torsam. Fond of cooking, he would get them to act as kitchen helpers while he made the meals. And they would talk squash, endlessly. Torsam's commitments as a player and coach left little time for holidays but he did manage to take his guests swimming quite often. Hassan and Zair then went back home while Jahangir stayed on to continue his training.

Torsam was a good coach, able to give his brother a hard game on the court, and Jahangir toughened up considerably. Friends were much impressed with his progress. Hiddy Jahan was one of them: 'The first time I ever saw that kid play in Pakistan, I knew he had the potential to make it. He was only very young then. In 1977 I remember saying that Jahangir would be dangerous within two years. It didn't take him that long. He had everything – at fifteen!'

Roshan had done all the groundwork with his younger son. It was left to Torsam to teach him about the practicalities of tournament play. Squash had undergone a transformation since the days of Khan rule in the fifties. In structure and organisation, the professional game had made considerable advances. The International Squash Rackets Federation was founded in 1967 to promote and control the game on a world-wide basis. Thanks to the initiative and drive of players like Jonah Barrington, the International Squash Players Professional Association came into being in 1973, later dropping the 'Professional' from its title to be known as ISPA.

Its stated aim was to protect the interests of its members and to 'liaise and work with all sports-governing bodies, tournament organisers and sponsors to further safeguard the development of professional squash throughout the world'. Ken Hiscoe was elected as its first President, Jonah Barrington was Chairman and Geoff Hunt was its Vice-President. Everyone found it much more convenient to have an organised body with whom they could now deal.

Jahangir had chosen the right time to arrive. Squash was flourishing at every level. New sponsors were coming into the game. More money was in circulation. The ranks of the professionals were swelling as a result. It would not be long before the distinctions between amateurs and professionals were abolished altogether. Squash was poised for even more exciting developments.

All this brought additional pressures for the players. To stand the pace of the larger circuit, they had to be much fitter in body and mind. Jet-setting was becoming the norm. As the global game expanded, every country was keen to see the world's best players. The demands made on them became heavier all the time. Torsam instructed his brother in how to cope with those pressures and demands. If he expected to make his living out of the game one day, he had to put in all the preparatory work.

Rahmat Khan's schedule showed how punishing the life of a professional could be. Five days a week, he taught at the Wembley Squash Centre. He helped to take Middlesex into the Premier Division and played in a series of exhibition matches all over the country. Along with Yasin, he was a main practice partner for the English Amateur Squash Team which was due to compete in the World Championships in Australia with

Barrington as its coach. Rahmat also reckoned to train at least four hours a day. Then there were tournaments: as well as taking part in British and European events, he travelled to Australia, New Zealand, South Africa, Canada, America and Pakistan. In a normal year he would expect to be away from home for up to five months. All this plus his business commitments with Unsquashable – it was no life of leisure.

Jahangir was not frightened by the commitment involved. He responded to the challenge with the single-mindedness that was to become his calling card. In April 1979, his power and variation took him to the final of the British Junior Open Championship where he lost to Glen Brumby of Australia, who was three years older. The Drysdale Cup had eluded him but he had got close enough to scent victory. It smelled good. He wanted to inhale more of its fragrance.

The next major challenge for him was the World Amateur Championships. Torsam pushed him relentlessly to get him in prime condition. Jahangir's strength and speed were causing problems for everybody, even Torsam himself. Rahmat, Yasin, Awad, Aziz, Asran, Abbas Khan and others gave him practice games. Whenever the boy had a particularly good run against this quality opposition, Torsam would ring up Hiddy Jahan: 'He's beating everyone. I'm sending him down so you can put him in his place.'

Jahangir would go to Croydon and take on the man who was number four in the world rankings. Even a powerhouse like Jahan had his work cut out to contain the young fireball. It was only a question of time before he came through with a real bang. The World Amateur gave him his chance. Torsam had high hopes for him but never believed he would actually win it. Then Jahangir beat Jonny Leslie of England, the favourite, and the odds against him shortened. Torsam and Rahmat now saw that he had a real opportunity of going all the way. In an interview, Rahmat predicted that Jahangir would become world champion.

His prediction might never have been made possible because Jahangir was very lucky to get to Australia in the first place. But for another slender thread of chance, he might not have taken part. He had been living in England for several months when he was recalled for the trials. He flew to Karachi, then on to Peshawar. He was not acclimatised and jet lag sapped him. Forced to play two and three matches a day, he was below par. He did not make the modest four-man team but they took him along as second reserve and told him that he would compete in the individual event.

When he reached Melbourne, however, he found to his chagrin that he had not been granted a place in the qualifying draw. He had come all that way to sit on the sidelines. Then another player withdrew and he was drafted in to fill the vacancy. Jahangir came through the qualifying rounds to secure a place in the main sixty-four man draw. There was still a long way to go but he showed his character by surviving a two-game deficit to win against Lars Kvant in the second round. It gave him extra confidence. He surged on, wearing down opponent after opponent until he reached the semi-final. He was due to meet Frank Donnelly, the Australian Amateur champion, seeded at number six.

Jahangir had beaten some good opposition but he had not done it alone. Torsam had been at the other end of a telephone in England, analysing his opponents for him, deciding on a match-plan, boosting his morale. He explained how Donnelly could be beaten and Jahangir followed his advice to the letter. He pinned the Australian at the back of the court and killed any loose returns with sweet drop shots. The Pakistani Whizz Kid, as he was dubbed by the local press, won in straight games, allowing Donnelly a miserly eleven points in a match that barely outlasted three-quarters of an hour. The rank outsider had reached the final of the World Amateur Championship. Torsam had switched Jahangir over from Dunlop rackets to those from the Unsquashable range. The youngster went into his first world final with a racket designed by his cousin, Rahmat.

His opponent was to be Phil Kenyon of England who had come through a long, tough semi-final with Atlas Khan, the so-called Machine Man from Peshawar. Torsam once again coached by remote control. He had only played Kenyon once but had seen him in action many times. The English player was a strong, seasoned twenty-three year old who was renowned for his fitness. He had the perfect build for squash, being of medium height with muscular legs that scurried at speed and with a compact torso that showed upper body strength. Kenyon already had a quiver-full of titles and he was favourite to win yet another.

Jahangir thought otherwise. It would be a difficult match but Torsam's counsel had given him ammunition, or so he hoped. When Kenyon got off to a blistering start, however, and took the first game 9–2, it looked as if the whizz kid had finally met his match. He was firing blanks. Jahangir removed the Stellar sponsorship shirt which he had been asked to wear and donned the national shirt which bore the star and the crescent moon of Pakistan. It was a symbol of patriotic endeavour. When he got back on court, he redoubled his efforts. Hitting a beautiful length, he extended the rallies until they began to tell on even Kenyon's stamina. Remorseless pressure gave him the next two games 9–3, 9–3. His opponent rallied in the fourth and quickened the pace but Jahangir matched it. Keeping the ball high and deep, he moved his man around all the time. Power and patience ultimately paid off. Jahangir won the game 9–5 to seal a quite astonishing victory.

Someone who was not even considered good enough to represent his country in the team event had taken on and beaten all-comers. He was only fifteen and he was champion of the world.

Phil Kenyon was naturally upset: 'I was disappointed to lose and I should have won, really. But I'd had a gruelling hour-and-a-half semi with Atlas Khan while Jahangir had an easy workout with Frank Donnelly. That's the way it goes. Jahangir played very well and I'd have had to be at my best to beat him.'

The champion himself confessed to some last-minute doubts. 'I was so nervous. I didn't believe I could win. I felt so lucky.'

When the news flashed around the squash world, it caused delight and disturbance. Torsam, Rahmat, Aman and their friends were overjoyed. Hiddy Jahan was pleased that his prediction had come true. But there were many players who were rocked by what they heard. If Jahangir Khan could win a world title at fifteen, what feats could he achieve when he grew up? The mind boggled.

Roshan Khan could not believe the announcement on his radio. He rang up the station in Karachi and asked for confirmation.

'Please. What you say about world squash championship. Please repeat it.'

'Who is this?' asked a voice.

'I am Roshan Khan, the father of Jahangir Khan.'

'Well, Roshan Khan, your son, Jahangir, has just won the world amateur title in Melbourne.'

'This is true?'

'Yes, sir. Congratulations.'

Roshan put down the receiver with tears of joy in his eyes. The delicate child with the double hernia had confounded them all. He was a true Pathan with a warrior's fighting instinct. He had flown off to Australia as a second reserve and was coming back with a world title.

Family celebrations were in order. The Khan dynasty was back in business.

DEATH AND REBIRTH

When Jahangir Khan won the championship point in Melbourne, he fell spontaneously to his knees in prayer. Allah had to be thanked first. Jahangir believed that only He could have made it all possible. The boy had precocious gifts which he developed with manic application but that was not enough. The will of Allah was paramount. Oblivious to the gathering pandemonium all around him, Jahangir shared his moment of triumph with his God.

When he got up off his knees again, he found that he was famous. Everyone wanted to congratulate him or ask him questions or take his picture or get his autograph. The media buzzed around him like hornets. It was midnight but the noonday sun of glory blazed down on him. It was his first experience of stardom. Almost as surprising as his success was his ability to cope with it. No boasting, no arrogance, he was calm and self-possessed. His English was halting but that did not matter. His performance had been eloquent.

He could not wait to get back to England to enjoy the reaction of Torsam and Rahmat and Aman. He was dying to speak to his father to tell him exactly how he had played. There was deep personal satisfaction in the win but he was gratified when he thought what it would mean to his family, his friends, his country. Pakistan amateurs were starved of competition and denied the best facilities. He had proved that the disadvantages could be overcome. He had pioneered a route that others might now be encouraged to take.

Torsam was waiting for him when he finally returned. It was a happy reunion with laughter and celebration for hours on end. His win was not an isolated fluke but a first giant step towards the top-most rung of the professional game. They fantasized about what the future would hold. They made plans, gave promises. Torsam had decided to retire from competitive play and devote himself to coaching his brother. He would play one last tournament. Fittingly, it would be down in Australia where Jahangir had just made squash history.

Torsam had accepted that he himself would never become the world's number one. It was time to step aside and let Jahangir take a shot at it. There was another new departure. With Rahmat and a friend, Torsam was hoping to take over Dunnings Mill Squash Club in Sussex. With their experience and know-how, they felt sure that they could make a success of it. They had many happy hours of discussion. Then Torsam set off for Australia. Jahangir would never see him alive again.

The tournament was the Australian Open and it was held at Brahma Lodge in Adelaide. Most of the world's best players were there. Torsam was only competing so that he could go out in triumph. He was desperate to improve his ranking. A good display in Adelaide would gain him the points that would move him up. He confided his decision to Hiddy Jahan: 'I owe you one, Hiddy. I'm going to give up the game. I'll train you and Jahangir so well that, by Christmas, no son-of-a-bitch will beat you.' It was typical stuff from Torsam – direct, honest and brimming with confidence.

When the tournament started, Torsam flung himself into it with controlled abandon. He met Ken Hiscoe in the first round and their match was amiably hostile. Now past forty, the Australian was not able to hold Torsam as he had done in the old days. The younger player progressed to the second round where he was due to meet Neven Barbour of New Zealand. Everyone expected Torsam to win and he entered the match with his spirits high.

The euphoria did not last. He soon found himself locked in another battle royal. Both players bumped and jostled and fought. They constantly got in each other's way. Torsam was hit hard on the jaw by Barbour's racket early on and had to rest for a minute or so. When play resumed, the struggle intensified. They pushed and shoved their way through a match that was

SHAPE OF THINGS TO COME.
This early duel between Jahangir and the bearded Ross Norman foreshadowed their long sequence
of battles.

(OPPOSITE TOP LEFT) PULLING POWER.
Rahmat and Jahangir play an exhibition
match in front of a full house.

(BOTTOM) OFF DUTY.
Friends relax during a break in
training. Left to right: Stuart Sharp,
Mo Yasin, Rahmat, Qamar Zaman,
Jahangir and Maqsood Ahmed.

(TOP RIGHT) UNSQUASHABLE.
Rahmat and Jahangir promote their
company at a trade exhibition.

(LEFT) THIS PAGE 10 DOWNING
STREET. Margaret Thatcher tries to
get a word in as Jahangir is greeted
by Mr Junejo, former Prime Minister
of Pakistan.

(BELOW) HORIZONTAL HOLD.
The immortal Hashim Khan takes a
breather on court.

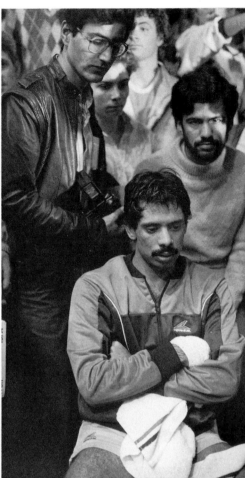

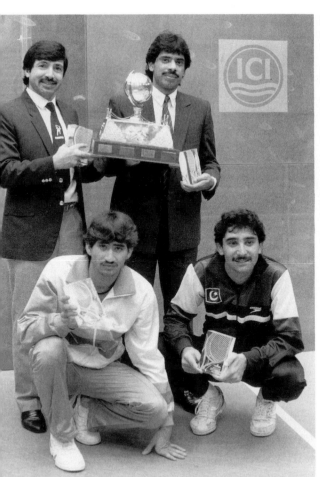

(OPPOSITE TOP LEFT) Rahmat with his daughter, Natasha. Is he holding the future of the women's game in his hands?

(TOP RIGHT) FACE OF DEFEAT.
Toulouse, 1986. Jahangir experiences the despair of losing his world title to Ross Norman.

(BOTTOM) VICTORY SALUTE.
After yet another British Open victory, Jahangir is besieged by autograph hunters.

(LEFT) THIS PAGE LAST NIGHT OF THE PROMS.
The Albert Hall echoed to a different kind of music in October 1987, when the World Team Championships were held there. Pakistan took the title, thanks to Qamar Zaman, standing with Jahangir; and Jansher Khan, reigning world champion, kneeling with Umar Hayat Khan.

(BELOW) PEP TALK.
Rahmat imparts words of wisdom to a perspiring Jahangir during the Monaco Open, 1988.

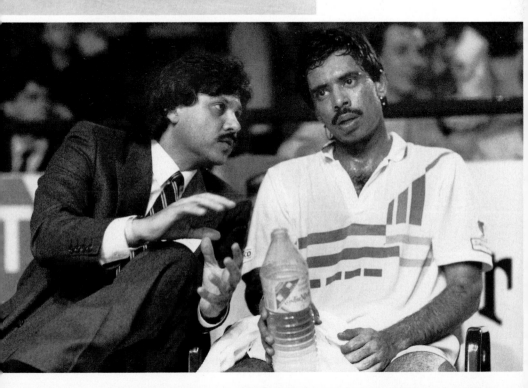

Jahangir in a reflective mood during the 1987 World Open Championships at the NEC in Birmingham.

Rahmat and Aman, a winning team as brothers and as coaches.

(TOP LEFT) Roshan Khan, centre right, is shown around the village of Nawakille by a relative. The houses are still as primitive as in his day.

(ABOVE) Josie Khan, Rahmat's wife.

(LEFT) Jahangir receives a kiss of encouragement from his niece, Natasha, before the 1981 World Open final in Toronto.

(BOTTOM) FAMILY ALBUM. Rahmat's children, Soraya, Tariq and Natasha.

(TOP LEFT) CONTINUING BATTLE.
The rivalry between Rahmat and Yasin as players was to continue when they became the coaches of Jahangir and Jansher, respectively.

(TOP RIGHT) TWO JK's. Jahangir Khan and Jansher Khan contest the semi-final of the 1987 World Open at Birmingham. Jansher won the match and went on to take the title.

(ABOVE) Torsam in action at the PIA Squash Complex in Karachi under the watchful eyes of (front row, left to right) Rahmat and Hiddy Jahan.

(BOTTOM RIGHT) Jahangir in full flight.

spoiled by flashes of temper and punctuated by let calls. It was fierce, uncompromising squash, played at high speed and with bruising commitment.

They had reached 6–6 when there was another collision. The New Zealander appealed for a let. Len Atkins, the referee, disallowed it and warned both players for playing too closely and not going for the ball. This official reprimand drew applause from the hundred-strong gallery. Tragedy then intervened.

Hiddy Jahan was an eye-witness to what happened. He had played in the previous game and taken a shower. When he returned to the court, Torsam was arguing with the referee: 'Suddenly, he collapsed. It wasn't a fall, he sort of sat down. His racket dropped out of his hand. We could all see that he was in serious trouble. Luckily, there were two doctors in the audience. One of them had helped to organise the tournament. They rushed on court. Gogi and I followed them.'

Torsam was lying on his side, his body limp, his eyes closed. The first doctor on the scene examined him carefully then turned him gently on to his back. He removed the player's shoes to give him air. Jahan was bending over his stricken friend when he seemed to rally slightly. His eyelids flicker-ed.

'What happened?' murmured Torsam. 'What happened?'

'Nothing happened,' soothed Jahan. 'You're not playing any more, that's all.'

Torsam winced as another spasm of pain hit him.

'It's coming again.'

He lapsed back into unconsciousness. His whole body was now shaking and the doctor put a hand in his mouth to stop him biting his tongue. A heart attack does not respect the decencies. Gogi Alauddin was shocked.

'That doesn't look very good,' he said anxiously.

The doctor tried mouth-to-mouth resuscitation and external heart massage but Torsam remained beyond his reach. Frozen in their seats, the spectators watched it all in horror. Neven Barbour was in a torment of guilt. He felt directly responsible. But he must be absolved of any blame. It was Torsam's own decision to enter the tournament. His love of the game was

115

greater than his fears about his physical condition. There had been warnings before but he had chosen to ignore them.

When the ambulance came, he was taken to the nearest hospital, the Lyell McEwin at Elizabeth Vale. Hiddy Jahan and Gogi Alauddin went with him and waiting for two hours while the staff tried to revive him. They were told that he would be moved to an intensive care unit in a bigger hospital if there was any hope. The doctors eventually decided that there was a slim chance of recovery but they put it no higher than twenty per cent. Jahan was in tears. He was still in mourning for the death of his mother. To lose such a close friend at this point would be unbearable.

Torsam was transferred to the Royal Adelaide and admitted to intensive care in a critical condition. He was put on a life support machine. Jahan was given the grisly task of passing on the news. He rang his wife, Susan, in England and explained the situation. He asked her to contact Rahmat: 'They won't believe it at first. Make them understand that Torsam might not be here tomorrow. It's that serious.'

Susan Jahan nerved herself to ring Rahmat: 'It was a dreadful thing to have to do. I felt awful. But the family had to be told.' As her husband had warned, Rahmat refused to believe it at first.

'Torsam's had these turns before,' he said.

'Not as bad as this.'

'He'll be okay,' added Rahmat, trying to reassure himself as much as anything. 'Torsam will come through.'

'They've put him on a life support machine.'

'Oh.'

Rahmat was stunned as he realised the implications.

'Hiddy says you're to ring the hospital and speak to the doctors. I've got the number for you . . .'

Rahmat immediately contacted Aman who caught the next train from Birmingham. He also rang the squash centre and asked Jahangir to come home at once. When he broke the terrible news, they were shattered. Torsam was so full of life and energy. The thought that it could all be extinguished so easily was appalling. Rahmat rang the Royal Adelaide Hospital and heard the prognosis from one of the doctors. Chances of recovery were very slim. Rahmat was advised to prepare himself for the worst. He put down the receiver in a state of shock.

Roshan was telephoned in Karachi. He was overwhelmed with helplessness. At a time when he most needed to be at his son's bedside, he was thousands of miles away. Rahmat, Aman and Jahangir felt the same. They wanted to be *with* Torsam, to help him fight, to will him back to life, to pray for him. All they could do was to wait. The hours passed with agonising slowness. Jahangir was desolate. In the previous month, Australia had blessed him with the bounty of a world title. Would it now exact a fearful payment? Did his brother *have* to die?

Torsam did improve slightly during the night but then suffered another attack. His condition was now hopeless. Massive brain damage had been caused by cardiac arrest. He would never recover. The doctors asked Hiddy Jahan for permission to turn off the life support machine. Jahan was quite unable to take such a decision. Only the family could do that. The hospital telephoned Rahmat in London and put the question to him but he could not give them permission. It was Roshan who had to make the grim choice.

Roshan listened to what the doctor had to say. Torsam was now beyond medical help. Effectively, his brain was dead. Without the life-support machine, his body would immediately cease to function. To all intents and purposes, there seemed no real choice. After long and troubled thought, Roshan accepted the inevitable. He gave permission for the doctors to turn off the machine. Torsam Khan had died.

Because no post mortems were held in Pakistan, the autopsy was held in Australia and this delayed the return of the body. Rahmat and Jahangir flew straight back to be with Roshan and the family. It was a sad homecoming. Nasrullah's death had been a fearful blow but he at least had lived out a reasonable span and been given the chance to fulfil his great potential. Torsam had been cut down in his prime. All his plans for the future now lay in ruins. There would be no partnership in a squash club, no coaching of his younger brother, no triumphs in which he could take his rightful share.

117

As the family reeled from the shock of it all, they were bound to look back at incidents from the past. There *had* been problems with Torsam's health but he always minimised them. Rahmat recalled a time at Edgbaston Priory a couple of years before. Torsam had complained of severe pains in his chest. An ambulance was called. While waiting for it to arrive, he was violently sick. Then he seemed to recover and the ambulance was sent away again. When Torsam saw a doctor, he was told that the attack might have been brought on by delayed shock because he had been involved in a car accident the same day.

There was an occasion in Canada when he had trouble breathing and had to be given oxygen. There were times when he had chest pains during a match or a practice session but passed them off as indigestion. Twelve months earlier, he had collapsed during a tournament in New Zealand but the doctors had discharged him with a clean bill of health. He had experienced further difficulties on this last trip to Australia. On the Saturday prior to the Australian Open, he withdrew from the Tea Tree Gully Open because of bouts of giddiness.

And yet he had gone on to play in the subsequent tournament. Was it bravery or folly? How much did Torsam know or suspect? Why did he take such an enormous risk? Did he live his life at such a hectic pace because of forewarning? Was he trying to cram experiences into the limited time that might be available to him? The answers will never be known but one thing is clear. He was an archetypal Khan. He loved squash with a passion that swept aside other considerations. His family lived for the game; he died for it.

During the delay in Australia, everyone connected with the tournament was sympathetic and helpful. Geoff Hunt gave enormous assistance, arranging for the body to be flown back to Pakistan. He had had some rare battles with Torsam himself and was deeply upset by his death. Later, Hunt and Bruce Brownlee, the New Zealand player, would help to organise a tournament for the Torsam Khan Cup. The Pakistani had always been popular with his fellow-players and had just been elected President of ISPA. It was a mark of the respect in which he was held. At the time of his death, he was ranked – unluckily – thirteenth.

118

Hiddy Jahan and Gogi Alauddin withdrew from the tournament. They were both too distressed to continue. Their thoughts were with Torsam, who had been such a dynamic personality on the circuit. When the body was released, Jahan accompanied it as far as Singapore. He arranged for a friend to travel with the coffin to Karachi. The death of his mother and Torsam within such a short span of time had jolted him to his foundations. The manner of Torsam's death continued to haunt him and it affected his own confidence on court. Whenever he got out of breath, he wondered if he had a weak heart and if he was putting his life at risk. Doctors reassured him that he was perfectly healthy but it took time to rebuild his confidence.

When the body arrived in Karachi, a family funeral was held. Relatives and friends came to pay homage to the memory of Torsam Khan and to pray for his soul. He was buried in one of the city's cemeteries. Roshan, Rahmat, Hassan and Jahangir adorned the grave with flowers. It was ironic. Jahangir had seemed so weak yet had emerged as a figure of exceptional strength; Torsam had appeared to be so strong but he was afflicted with a fatal weakness.

The whole family were numbed by what had happened. Jahangir was pole-axed: 'When my brother died, I had really big shock. I just gave up squash for two or three months. Just don't want to play any more, you know. Sometimes he come in a dream, you know, when I am sleeping. Torsam comes in a dream, telling me about squash and we playing together and laughing and I want to see him again.'

Rahmat was aware of how his young cousin felt: 'I looked at Jahangir. He was sitting there, a little kid of fifteen, probably wondering if his future was in danger. What was going to happen to him? And that made me think. Maybe that could be the meaning of *my* life.' Nasrullah's death had brought about a change in Rahmat. He viewed things in a much more serious light and became more devout in his religious observances. During his early years in Britain, he had been something of a playboy, a carefree man-about-town who had enjoyed the fruits of a Western society. That had been severely modified. He had married and settled down. The loss of Torsam only

119

served to reinforce the decisions he had made about the sort of life he would live. Perhaps he could take over the coaching of Jahangir and achieve the bold targets that Torsam had set. It was a challenge he felt impelled to accept.

He discussed the matter with Roshan. When a decent interval had passed, Jahangir was sounded out: 'But then later, the family members and other people says to me that it was Torsam's ambition to make me world number one. Why didn't I carry on with that?' In his dejection, the young player could not at first raise much enthusiasm for squash. It had claimed his brother's life and robbed him of his desire to play. There was another consideration. If he was to continue with his playing career, should he go to Britain or remain in Pakistan?

This was not just a family decision. It was a matter of national importance. Jahangir Khan was world amateur champion. If he was coached correctly and if he dedicated himself sufficiently, there was a possibility that he might win the professional crown. That would be a matter for national celebration.

Four people came together to talk it over. Roshan, Rahmat, Brigadier Artif and Retired Air Marshall Nur Khan, the whirring dynamo behind the development of PIA's sponsorship of the sport. What was the best thing for Jahangir? To go with Rahmat or to be coached by someone else in his own country? Roshan wanted him at home. The loss of one son had drawn him closer to the other two. Besides, a male child represented earning potential in Pakistan. A poor family like theirs needed all the help it could get from its members. Jahangir would be of more direct use if he remained at home.

The top brass from PIA agreed with this. Brigadier Artif and Nur Khan advanced two more arguments. If Jahangir went to London, he was in danger of being corrupted by Western values. There had been further political changes in Pakistan. Mr Bhutto was executed in April 1979, to be succeeded by General Zia-el-Haq. The new dispensation was running every-thing with military thoroughness and there was a steady swing towards fundamentalist Islamic rule. Jahangir Khan was a Muslim. It would be wrong to subject him to the temptations of a more lax society like that of Britain.

In practical terms, they added, it might not work out. Apart from Hiddy Jahan, none of the British-based Pakistani players had made it to the top of the ranking list. Torsam had been there for nine years without achieving the real breakthrough. Rahmat had lived there even longer but had yet to get into the top ten. There were other examples. Home-based players like Zaman, Alauddin and Mohibullah junior were far more successful. They drew strength from their roots.

Rahmat heard them out then stated his case. He believed that Jahangir could only become world champion if he moved to London where he would get the finest training facilities and the highest standard of playing partners. The boy had not been corrupted by the West so far, yet he had lived there for several months. Rahmat promised to shield him from all temptation and to bring him up in the Muslim religion to which he himself was now more ardently committed.

The discussion went on for a long time. In the end, the burden of decision rested on Roshan. He was the boy's father. It was up to him to decide his son's future. Roshan weighed up all the arguments on their own merits. His heart wanted Jahangir to stay but his head told him that he should be allowed to go. Rahmat was not just the best coach for him, he was the *only* coach. As a member of the family, he understood the nature of its traditions. As Jahangir's elder cousin, he commanded automatic respect from the boy. As a top-flight player in his own right, he knew what the life of a professional entailed. And as Nasrullah's son, he was touched with coaching genius.

There was another telling point. Rahmat was married so could offer Jahangir the comfort and security of a family home. It would be an effective barrier against the social evils of the decadent West. The boy would be at the very centre of the squash world. No other country could compete with Britain in terms of facilities. That was where the real action was.

The decision was made. Rahmat would take over from Torsam. It was no light undertaking. Nur Khan emphasized the fact: 'You are responsible, Rahmat, because if he was here, it's fortunate for us that he's a national asset. In three years – though he's still very young yet – but in three years, he should

121

be good enough to beat Hunt. If you take him, the responsibility to the nation is yours.'

The scene would have been unimaginable in any other country. None of them prioritised squash to such a degree. Jonah Barrington's career was never discussed at a family meeting with the top brass of British Airways. Politics did not intrude into Geoff Hunt's thinking about the game that he dominated. Potential world champions in other countries were not singled out to bear such a crushing weight of national expectation. Coaches elsewhere were not given the choice between producing a world champion or being branded as a failure.

Yet it all seemed perfectly natural in Pakistan. International sport was viewed with high seriousness. Another world-beater from the Khan family would have untold propaganda value. Rahmat understood all this and did not flinch from its implications. He had the courage and the vision to chart a path for Jahangir. As long as the boy agreed to obey him at all times, Rahmat was certain that Torsam's hopes for him could in time be realised. Nur Khan had given him three years. If it meant sacrificing his own playing career, so be it. Rahmat was ready to do anything to fulfil his responsibility.

Jahangir was told about the decision and he accepted it. Some of his enthusiasm for the game had died along with Torsam but it was to be rekindled. All his ambitions would be reborn and given new definition. Player and coach vowed that they would succeed together. They owed it to their family and to their country. It was a sacred mission. Winning the world championship would be the finest gift that Jahangir could present at the grave of his brother. He embarked on his quest.

When they got back to London, there were problems of adjustment. Josie Khan had given birth to a daughter, Natasha, the previous autumn. Rahmat's wife had to cope with an additional member of the family now. By the same token, Jahangir had to learn to fit in at the Wembley flat. It would be very different from his days with Torsam down in Sutton. Fortunately, the flat had three bedrooms so the newcomer could have a room of his own. Showing him into it, Rahmat placed a photograph of Torsam by the bedside. It was intended to remind Jahangir of his pledge to realise his brother's high hopes for him. It would be an inspiration.

Rahmat made another point. The room in which Jahangir would sleep was not only a place of peace and prayer. It was shaped like a squash court. When the boy looked up from the bed, he could imagine the angles at which a rubber ball would bounce off. By letting his fantasies roam, he could also help to master the geometry of the game. From the start, Rahmat treated his guest with the brisk affection of an older brother. They had always been good friends. It was vital now to establish a deeper trust between them. Torsam's death had brought them together and given them a sense of unity. That bond had to be reinforced.

By way of illustration, Rahmat handed Jahangir a squash racket.

'Break it,' he suggested.

'The racket?'

'Snap it in two.'

It was a strange request and it made Jahangir smile but he did as he was told. Putting it across his knee, he proved that Unsquashable rackets were not unbreakable. It snapped under pressure.

Rahmat now gave him two more rackets from stock.

'Break these.'

'Both of them?' asked Jahangir, curious to know why Rahmat was asking him to destroy perfectly good equipment.

'Hold them together.'

Jahangir once again obeyed and placed the rackets across his knee. But the resistance was too great now. Though he applied his full force, he could only bend the rackets slightly. He gave up.

'It's impossible,' he admitted.

'Remember that,' urged Rahmat, 'It is easy to break one but it is difficult to break two. And if we stick together, nobody will be able to break us.'

It was a simple lesson but the point was driven home.

Jahangir's life was now divided between three main venues – the Wembley Squash Centre, the flat and the mosque. Rahmat was much more than just a coach. He was a mentor, language teacher, landlord, religious instructor, business advisor and companion. Honesty was the basis of their relationship. Nothing was to be kept hidden. Jahangir was to do everything he was asked. If he did not or could not, he was to admit it. Rahmat stressed the importance of training. Stamina was mandatory. A big building had to have strong foundations. It was the same with a world champion squash player. He had to build brick by brick. Each day of the training schedule would add another row of bricks.

Jahangir did not adapt to his new home overnight. Though he had been in England before, he still experienced culture shock. The language, climate, food and people were so different from Pakistan. He felt homesick. He also cried when he thought of Torsam. One day Rahmat put a stop to this. No matter how hard it was for Jahangir, he had to hold back his tears. They were a sign of weakness. He must show strength. Torsam had to be a positive factor in his life.

Training was hard. Rahmat was a demanding coach and he drove his cousin on. There was leeway to make up. During his time in Pakistan, the boy had not touched a squash racket. He was unfit and had lost his competitive edge. Rahmat had him running, weight-training and working out on court. Practice matches were long and taxing. By the time they got back to the flat in the evenings, the boy was exhausted. But he was regaining his zest for the game. The unrelenting slog was a kind of therapy. It stopped him from brooding about Torsam.

Everything was geared towards the British Amateur Championship. Torsam's plan had been for him to take the title and then turn professional. Jahangir fell at the first hurdle. On the eve of the event, he was having a practice hit with Karimullah when he slipped and strained his back. Rahmat took him to the physiotherapist at once and the news was bad. The injury would put him out of action for some time. If he took part in the championship, he could be risking his whole playing career. They had to swallow their disappointment and withdraw. Jahangir's chance of taking the British Amateur title had gone forever; he announced that he was turning professional.

When he was able to train again, he tried to put the upset

behind him and concentrate on doing well in his first tournament on the professional circuit. It was the ISPA Championship, an event which had only been running for two years but which attracted a tough field. Southampton was the venue that year. Jahangir was drawn against Hiddy Jahan. Off court, the older player was charming and affable but when the match started, he became ruthless. Jahan was the complete professional. He did nobody any favours on court.

It was the biggest test Jahangir had ever faced and he did not let himself down. Though he was beaten in the end, he had put up noble resistance and given one of the world's finest players a run for his money. The score was 9–7, 1–9, 9–4, 7–9, 0–9. There were not many players who took twenty-six points off Jahan the first time they met him in a tournament. It was an accomplished display and the forthright Jahan was the first to acknowledge it: 'He bloody well played well. Jahangir will be world champion in two years!'

It was a bold prediction but not the first he had made. Jahan had forecast the young Pathan's win in the World Amateur even though he had not even been selected for the Pakistan team. Would his crystal ball work again this time? Or was it clouded by his love and loyalty for Torsam? Most experts were in frank disagreement with the claim. They estimated that it would take Jahangir five years to get to the top. Rahmat supported Jahan's prediction. When asked about the opinion of other observers, he had a short answer: 'That is their thinking and this is our faith.'

That faith took something of a pounding a couple of months later. Jahangir lost to Gawain Briars of England, Ali Aziz of Egypt, Jonah Barrington of Ireland and Gogi Alauddin of Pakistan. In the final of the Irish Open in May 1980, he was again torpedoed by the greater court craft of Barrington. There was a lesson to be drawn from the defeats. Jahangir had ability enough but his stamina was inadequate. He could not stand the pace in a long match. Rahmat was stern with him. When he lost to Briars in four games, the coach took Jahangir to a practice court and gave him the fifth game he had not played.

The season was over but the treadmill did not stop. If anything it was speeded up in a search to eliminate the weaknesses from his game. To strengthen his legs, he was running twenty quarter-miles with only a brief respite between each lap. There were even times when Rahmat made him run while holding on to his back. Most players would have protested about that but Jahangir honoured his promise and made no complaint. His stamina improved and his confidence swelled.

When the new season got under way, the first major event was the Schweppes World Open in Australia. Jahangir travelled to Adelaide with mixed feelings. It was the place where Torsam had lost his life. He put this out of his mind when the tournament started and sailed through the first two rounds, beating Massey and Yeates, both of Australia. Maqsood Ahmed was his victim in the third round; then he took on the great magician himself, Qamar Zaman. The former world champion won but he had been taken to five games. Jahangir's form had definitely improved.

This was underlined when he went on to win the New Zealand Open, accounting for Ross Norman, Gamal Awad and Bruce Brownlee in the process. It was a good win but most of the leading professionals were absent. Jahangir had still not proved himself in a really testing final. His opportunity came in Karachi later that autumn. He reached the final of the PIA Masters at a gallop, even disposing of the tricky Mohibullah junior in the semi-final. He now faced Qamar Zaman for the second time. The championship court at the PIA Squash Complex was bursting at the seams. Roshan and Hassan were there to cheer him on. The PIA top brass were there to assess his progress. Rahmat was there to advise him between games. The media were there to sit in judgement.

Jahangir did not disappoint them. Though he lost the first two games to the shimmering brilliance of Zaman, he surged back to take the last three games for a loss of only nine points. Against Zaman! It was sweet revenge for his defeat in the World Open and his first major title. He had won a signal victory in the place where it mattered most – in front of his father and in front of his home crowd.

Rahmat was the first to congratulate him.

'Well done, boy! You worked hard to get here.'

'I know,' gasped the other.

'This is only the start. Next target is British Under-23 Open. You will work even harder.'

Jahangir was ready for anything now. He had come to terms with the death of his brother. He had adapted to life in Britain. He had overcome his early setbacks in the professional circuit.

His love of the game had revived. A champion was reborn.

CONQUEROR OF THE WORLD

The new year got off to a flying start when Jahangir won the British Under-23 Open without relinquishing a game. Since it was held at Wembley, it was virtually on his doorstep. He dispatched Jaski, Lee and Willstrop of England in the first three rounds for an aggregate loss of only sixteen points. Holmes of South Africa was next to fall; then Zahir Husain Khan was toppled in the semi-final. Jahangir then played what was to be the first of a long chain of finals against the fair-haired Ross Norman. The slim, sinewy New Zealander had the appearance and aggression of a young Viking but it was not his day for pillage. Jahangir was the plunderer, keeping him under constant pressure and wresting the points from him. It was a fine performance and it made his critics sit up. Maybe that two-year prediction by Rahmat and Hiddy Jahan had not been so fanciful after all.

Richard Eaton of the *Sunday Times* had always taken it seriously. One of the shrewdest observers of the squash scene, he described Jahangir as the heir presumptive. In an article published in November 1980, he forecast that Jahangir might not manage to lower Hunt's colours in the next British Open but that he might well relieve him of the world title in Canada in a year's time. The heir presumptive was now starting to look like the heir apparent.

At a smaller tournament in Brussels in February, Jahangir collected another win by beating the powerful Bruce Brownlee. Later the same month at Edgbaston Priory, he won the final of the Prodorite Invitation Tournament by beating the flying grasshopper, Gamal Awad. Not even the rubber-legged acrobatics of the Egyptian could contain him. Jahangir was unstoppable and Rahmat was delighted by a win on a court that held so many fond memories for him. The spirit of Naz seemed to hover over the event.

His real chance was to come in March during the Canada Club Cup. It was held in Munich, a city which had already seen more than its share of sporting upsets. Gamal Awad stood between Jahangir and a place in the final against Geoff Hunt. In an energetic and always entertaining match, the Pakistani kept the upper hand throughout, never taking chances, never even giving a hint of youthful indiscretion. His maturity and discipline were striking. They earned him his first crack at the world champion. A full appraisal of Jahangir's potential could at last be made.

Hunt had been in his thoughts since the days when he had been coached by his father. He had a deep respect for the Australian and had studied his game with great care. Superior stamina was the only way to take out a man whose feats had now given him almost mythic status. That was why Rahmat had cracked the whip over him. The training schedule was intimidating. Every day except Sunday, Jahangir was out of bed at six o'clock to run ten miles before breakfast. Then he walked across to the squash centre and spent an hour on court alone, going through drills and exercises, adding precision and polish. After lunch and a rest, he practised with Rahmat. They played hard, long rallies that were peppered with advice and exhortation. Jahangir would then play a series of forty-five minute matches against top players. The day's work ended with light exercises and half an hour in the swimming pool.

It was not unrelieved slog. Rahmat knew how to introduce variation and light relief. He kept Jahangir's motivation high. The seventeen-year old was becoming a master of technique and tactics. He was as fit as a boxer before a big fight. Rahmat was the first to remind him of the similarity between the two sports: 'Squash is just like boxing. You have to learn to ride punches and hit back harder with counter-punches. The only difference is that the bruises are on the inside.'

Jahangir was excited by the chance to get in the ring with Hunt. It would be at once an honour and a supreme challenge. Hunt himself relished the clash. The name of Jahangir Khan had been thrown at him many times in articles and interviews. It was time to prove that he was still the undisputed king. Even though he was exactly twice the age of his opponent, he was not ready to abdicate just yet. The heir apparent had to be forcibly reminded of the fact.

The advantage, however, lay with Jahangir. Ambition burned inside him like a forest fire. He was at peak fitness. Hunt, on the other hand, had not fully recovered from jet lag after his flight from Australia. He was there for the taking. It was never going to be easy. With one foot nailed to the floor of the court, Hunt would still be a daunting opponent. But a performance of controlled power and patience by Jahangir could unsettle him, and so it did. It took four long, enervating, attritional games but the younger player did it. He beat the world champion 3–1. His delight was understandable. The result was a portent.

Within ten days, Hunt came back with a vengeance. They met in the final of the ISPA Smirnoff Masters which was held in Bangor, near Belfast. Jahangir for once tried to force the pace and go for his shots. He took far too many risks and paid the price. Hunt pounced on his mistakes with merciless savagery. Jahangir lost in straight games. It was a painful body blow to his morale. He had hoped to capitalise on his success in Germany. Had that really been such a freak occurrence? It was a case of back to the drawingboard. Rahmat had to prepare his plan of campaign for the next scheduled encounter – at the Patrick International Festival Tournament down in Chichester.

They took stock of their situation. Enormous strides had been made in the last year. Torsam's death had left a terrifying emptiness in Jahangir's life. That had now been filled. Rahmat had found the way to turn despair into dedication, to rebuild the shattered dreams of the young teenager. There had been setbacks but they had been surmounted. In 1981 Jahangir had become an irresistible force – until he got to Northern Ireland. The immoveable object named Geoffrey Brian Hunt came off best in the collision.

Rahmat endured a lot of sniping criticism after the result in Bangor. He was accused of trying to take his player too far too fast. It was suggested in some quarters that he might not be the best coach for Jahangir at all. This was not a new charge. From the moment that he had won the World Amateur, Jahangir had become a hot property. After Torsam's death, there were many people only too willing to take charge of his career, including Jonah Barrington. When Jahangir returned to London and took up squash again, he was watched with interest by all the top players. Many tackled him in practice matches, keen to see how well he was doing and what kind of threat he posed.

Jonah Barrington was among these players. He telephoned Rahmat and asked if he could come to Wembley and get on court with Jahangir. Coach and player were thrilled. For a man of Barrington's eminence to request a game was a boost to their ego. And he was prepared to travel down to *them*. It showed the high regard in which he held Jahangir. After a while, however, there was a change of tactic. Barrington rang Rahmat one day and asked if Jahangir could possibly go up to Birmingham to play. He was duly sent off on the train.

When Jahangir arrived for his work-out on court, however, the gallery was sprinkled with reporters. He was interviewed and photographed. Jahangir was taken aback by it all. He told Rahmat about it but the latter was not displeased. Barrington was doing them a favour by promoting the new star. It was all to the good.

They quickly revised this opinion when articles appeared which seemed to imply that Barrington was now coaching Jahangir. Friends asked Rahmat why he had stopped looking after his cousin. Enemies asked the same question in a less pleasant manner. It was at once embarrassing and annoying. Rahmat went into print with a categorical affirmation that he was Jahangir's only coach. The player himself confirmed this in unequivocal terms: 'I have only ever been coached by three people. My father, my brother, my cousin. Rahmat Khan is now my coach.' Young and rather naive, Jahangir felt that he had been taken advantage of in Birmingham. What was surprising was the fact that the person responsible was one of the all-time greats of squash.

Barrington's interest lingered. When Jahangir suffered his traumatic defeat at the hands of Hunt in Northern Ireland, he was approached by Madeline Barrington who put it to him that her husband might be a better coach for him. This was no discreet offer: it was made in front of Rahmat himself, Richard Eaton and Stuart Sharp, another member of the Khan camp. Jahangir was very angry. Rahmat was deeply insulted. It made for a cooling of relations with Jonah Barrington. Like father, like son. The rift in the lute has never been fully repaired. As late as 1987, Malcolm Hamer, former manager of Barrington, could refer to Rahmat as 'Jahangir's so-called coach'. This is rather like saying that Torvill was Dean's so-called ice-dance partner.

Documentary evidence is there in abundance. Stuart Sharp actually made a film of Jahangir's career, charting his rise from young hopeful to megastar. Sharp was a Midland businessman who first met Rahmat at the Squash Leicester club when he was there with Torsam. A dapper figure with an Imperial beard, Sharp was a keen squash player who reached county standard. In 1978 he got his first glimpse of Jahangir when the latter was playing a practice match with Rahmat at Wembley. That moment was to transform his whole life.

Sharp talks about a recurring dream that he had been having. He would encounter a young man with such a glow about him, such a halo effect, that Sharp felt compelled to follow. Almost like a disciple. When he first set eyes on Jahangir, he recognised him as the person in the dream: 'There was a kind of aura, an inner serenity that those who were perhaps too close to him had not noticed.' It exerted a powerful pull on Sharp. When his marriage broke up some time later, he wanted to leave Leicester and its associations. He needed a decisive change of direction. So he conceived the idea of making a film about Jahangir Khan. He discussed it with Rahmat and with Jahangir himself and they agreed.

Realising his business assets, Sharp invested the money in a film camera and moved to Wembley. He was not just going to be a fly on the wall of the squash court. He was another member of the family. Moving in to the spare room at the flat, he became one more factor in the equation. With no previous experience as a film cameraman, he made it up as he went along and learned the trade by trial and error. Some of the resulting footage is quite extraordinary. Sharp filmed *everything*.

No sportsman has ever had such comprehensive coverage of his career.

Stuart Sharp soon became a familiar figure on the circuit. With his chirpy manner and consuming interest in the sport, he made a real impact, especially when he wore the white suit that became something of a trade mark. The press corps gave him the affectionate nickname of Cecil B. DeMille but his film had no cast of thousands, just two players on a bare court engaged in a private melodrama. There would be times when the camera was a nuisance and an intrusion but Rahmat and Jahangir still permitted the film to roll.

When Jahangir had his third and most important match against Hunt at the Chichester Festival Theatre, Sharp was there with his equipment. He was to film a historic contest: Pakistan versus Australia, no holds barred. The match was a dress rehearsal for the British Open which was only a week away. Rahmat Khan would later describe it as the greatest exhibition of squash he had ever seen. Both he and Jahangir had been wounded by the comments made after the defeat in Northern Ireland. Their partnership had come under intense fire and here was the opportunity to vindicate it. Rahmat gave his instructions: 'Speak for both of us out there on the court. You know what to say.'

Their preparation had been meticulous. In the two previous matches with Hunt, they noticed that he seemed to tire after about fifty minutes. If there was a weakness there, it had to be exploited. Jahangir was told to keep him on court long enough and he would crack. Hunt's own preparation had also been meticulous. He did not underestimate his young opponent but got himself in prime condition. He wanted to show that he was still bull of the herd.

The two players locked horns with shuddering force. Hunt tried everything in his vast repertoire. He altered pace, angle and trajectory. He pushed Jahangir to the back of the court, then had him racing up to the front wall. For his part, Jahangir covered everything that came his way, throwing himself about with a reckless disregard of his stamina. Hunt used more economy of effort but the sheer speed of the match was taking its toll. The turning-point came in the fourth game when Hunt was leading 4–1. Suddenly, he began to weaken. Jahangir took full advantage and won eight points in a row to take the game.

Jahangir raced to a 5–1 lead in the deciding game and thought that he was home and dry. But Hunt drew on his capacious reserves of energy and experience to level the score at 6–6. The effort finished him: his arm went, his racket flailed around ineffectually, his legs turned to jelly. He was dead but just did not know how to lie down. Jahangir pressed on to win a memorable match that had lasted two hours and eleven minutes. Both of them had gone through the pain barrier to the frontiers of collapse. They were grey, haggard, exhausted, but they had served up a magnificent feast of squash.

Rahmat's advice had been sound. Hunt did finally give way under pressure. Player and coach had been vindicated. The Australian put on a brave face after the ordeal, then had a brief word alone with Jahangir. He conceded that the Pakistani had done to him what he had done to others, assassinated them in front of a paying audience. It took a lot to admit that. Jahangir's respect for Geoff Hunt was increased even more.

Attention now focussed on the forthcoming British Open which had a special significance. Having won the event seven times to equal the record of Hashim Khan, Hunt was now trying to surpass it. After the match with Jahangir in Northern Ireland he was the firm favourite, but Chichester altered that. More than one pundit was tipping the Pakistani. He not only had youth on his side, he had a family record to defend. That would put extra steel in his game.

The Audi British Open was held in the Churchill Theatre at Bromley in Kent, the county in which Hunt's father had been born. It was to prove a lucky omen. Buoyed up by his victory at Chichester, Jahangir was looking forward to another marathon against Hunt but he first had to reach the final. There were some tough opponents in his half of the draw, but he was in fine fettle. He saw off Mike Sherren of Zimbabwe, Sohail Qaisir of Pakistan, Dean Williams of Australia, Hiddy Jahan and – for the third time in a month – Qamar Zaman. As he hacked out his trail of terror, he did not lose a single game.

Conditions were very different to Chichester. The artificial court, which had been set up on stage, felt strange. The atmosphere was much tenser. Jahangir sensed right away that the bulk of the support was for Hunt, the reigning champion. Most people wanted to see him make squash history by taking his eighth title. Jahangir was the outsider, the callow usurper who was trying to seize the throne. He was very aware of the crowd feeling. It made him so nervous that he was trembling when he came on court for the knock-up.

The tactics were to be the same as at Chichester. Stretch Hunt until he began to crack. Keep the ball in play, maintain pressure in the rallies but have something in reserve for a fighting finish. Everyone knew that it would be a long match. There was no question of it being settled in three games. It was evenly balanced.

Geoff Hunt did not make the mistakes of the earlier match. He was calmer, more positive, more consistent. It was Jahangir who was forced into uncharacteristic errors. The games were endless and drained the vitality of both men. But it was Hunt who had the edge. He gave himself a useful cushion of two games. Jahangir replied by taking the third game and then moving on to a 6–1 lead in the fourth. It looked as if he would level the match. Hunt's resistance had weakened visibly. Was he already beaten or merely taking a breather?

Jahangir soon got his answer and it took him completely by surprise. Hunt had been conserving his strength for one last all-out attack. He produced a sustained burst of magical squash to overhaul his opponent and win 9–7. At two hours and fourteen minutes, the game was even longer than the Chichester battle. Hunt had the psychological boost of victory to take some of the ache out of his limbs but Jahangir was devastated. He felt that he had thrown away his chances in the last game. He had tried to finish the match too quickly and been chastised. Hunt had crowned a wonderful career by setting an apparently unbeatable record. It had been yet another classic.

Rahmat showed his quality as a coach. Instead of reproaching Jahangir, he congratulated him warmly and told him that he had played a fantastic game. Roshan later telephoned to add his felicitations. He was proud of his son. Both men knew that the player needed help and sympathy at this moment of crisis. He must not be made to feel that he had failed. From every game, there was something positive to take. Aman was on hand with persuasive tongue. What did it matter if Hunt had won eight British Opens? He was thirty-four and nearing the end of his reign. By the time Jahangir reached that age, he might have won *sixteen* British Opens on the trot!

But the player was still heartbroken. When the tears came, he begged Stuart Sharp to switch off the camera. He did not want his grief recorded on film. But the camera kept rolling. It was there to tell the full truth. Jahangir had played well but Hunt was better on the day. There would be other matches between them. If Jahangir felt demoralised by defeat then he would fight that much harder to avoid it next time. Those around the losing finalist hid their disappointment behind wise words and sympathy. Jahangir was not to feel ashamed.

He took comfort from the gracious words that Geoff Hunt had spoken about him into the microphone: 'Thanks very much, Jahangir. Not often that you play a player who's as fair as he is. Plays the game hard and tough but, on the other hand, he's always willing to call the balls not up and play a fabulous game. I've had some tremendous games with him already and I think a lot of his attitude on court. His dedication is due to his mentor and coach, Rahmat Khan, who's done a lot for him over the years and certainly is producing – along with Jahangir – a magnificent champion.' It takes one to know one.

The season was now over and it was time for a holiday. After the long round of tournaments and training sessions, Jahangir had earned a rest. With their intrepid cameraman in tow, he and Rahmat flew home to Pakistan to spend some time with the family. The lapping warmth of Karachi was very seductive after the crispness of April in Britain. They relaxed, they unwound, they recharged their batteries. Rahmat made no mention of Jahangir's errors in the British Open. He saved his criticism until the holiday was over. There would be time enough then. Jahangir was restored and refreshed by the rest. When he had to resume training, he did so with a zestful willingness.

They were flown to Gilgit in the north of the country by a PAF C130 transport plane. Jet aircraft could not land there because it was too dangerous. The entire Gilgit-Hunza area was in the shadow of high mountains. Only a small plane could swoop down between the peaks and land on the small runway. Rahmat and Jahangir were above the snow-line. It was the ideal place for high altitude training. The rugged conditions were a challenge, the air was bracing and the mountainous terrain formed a spectacular backdrop. Gilgit was rather short of squash courts but they were there to build up fitness. Jahangir ran every day to put strength in his legs and did programmes of exercises.

It was the beginning of a period of extensive training in preparation for the World Open at the end of November. Jahangir had to be in better shape than ever if he wanted to lift the title from Hunt. After a lengthy stay in Gilgit, they flew to Sweden for some more high altitude work. Then it was on to Australia to play some challenge matches with Hunt. The training did not slacken. Rahmat wanted to build both his mental and physical toughness.

The spiritual dimension of their lives was not forgotten. Five times a day – on rising, at noon, mid-afternoon, at sunset and before retiring – they spread out their prayer mats and knelt down facing Mecca. Stuart Sharp filmed it all but he was no objective observer. The more he saw of Islam in action, the more drawn he was towards it. Rahmat and Jahangir never took anything for granted. The word most frequently on their lips was 'Inshallah' – God willing. All the training in the world would not help them unless they had the blessing of Allah.

Sharp was fascinated. He began to discuss the basics of Muslim theology with Rahmat who was himself an enthusiastic student. Passages from the Koran were read and studied. Sharp was surprised at the amount of overlapping there was with the Christian Bible. He had always dismissed Islam as weird mumbo-jumbo in the past but it improved on acquaintance. And there was no gainsaying the effect it had on the lives of his two friends. It shaped their whole existence and gave them the impressive commitment which enabled them to pursue their training programme. Two major transformations were taking place.

While the losing finalist in a British Open was being turned into a potential world champion, the man behind the camera was slowly being converted to Islam. Rahmat found all his answers in the Koran: 'It tells me everything – even about how to approach squash.' Sharp was to find its appeal growing all the time. In retreat from the rat race of business, he was living with people who had a spiritual value in their daily existence. He followed where they led.

When the new season started, all the tournaments were viewed as warm-ups before the World Open in Canada. Jahangir started as he meant to go on. He beat Hiddy Jahan in an International Championship at Welwyn Garden City and then defeated him in the final of the Welsh Open at Swansea. The second event was to take on significance. It was the last time that Jahangir was taken to five games for several years. His unbeaten run had started.

The Asian Championships took them back to Karachi in October and gave Roshan a chance to see his son in action. He was thrilled when Jahangir trounced Qamar Zaman in the final. The latter was only able to mount a challenge in the first game which he lost 10–8. He did not score another point in the match. So much for the argument that home-based players had the advantage over Pakistani exiles. Zaman was one of the game's greatest ever strokeplayers yet the seventeen-year old Jahangir could now beat him as a matter of course.

Next stop was Cologne for the German Masters. Jahangir was in a mean mood when he took on Phil Kenyon, the man he had vanquished in the World Amateur back in 1979. The scoreline of 9–0, 9–1, 9–1 tells its own story. Gamal Awad and Hiddy Jahan also fell to the Khan racket; then he had his best moment of the new season when he defeated Geoff Hunt 3–1. It healed some of the wounds that still smarted from Bromley.

Newcastle was the next port of call. The Thorn EMI Heating World Masters' Tournament threw Jahangir up against Zaman yet again. The contrast in their styles always made for spectator interest and Zaman was in spirited form. When he had claimed the first game, however, he was shut off completely. The next three games only yielded him a total of four points. Five wins in five tournaments and another victory over Hunt. It was an ideal build-up to the ultimate test.

Toronto hosted the 1981 World Open Championship. The

event was now in its fifth year. It was gathering momentum and prestige all the time. A Pakistani player had contested the final for each of the four years but Hunt had always beaten them. Mohibullah had been repelled once and Zaman had lost three times in a row. Jahangir vowed that he would not be a losing finalist as well – Inshallah. It was almost two years since Torsam's death. Time to fulfil the prediction.

The McGuinness World Open was held in a modern squash complex with good facilities. The Canadians gave their guests a cordial welcome and a friendly atmosphere prevailed throughout the championship. Jahangir, Rahmat, his wife and daughter were staying at the Holiday Inn. Stuart Sharp had a disturbing habit of popping up in their rooms with his camera – The Eye That Never Sleeps. He was anxious to film the off-court moments as well as the actual play.

Sharp's own judgement was now on trial. If his instinct had been right and Jahangir *did* win, then his film would have a superb climax. He had banked everything on the success of the young man with the aura. But supposing he failed? Supposing Hunt beat him? Supposing he got injured in some way? Supposing a third person emerged at the championship to steal the title from both of them? Sharp's presence had not always been welcomed by some of the players. Petty jealousies led to some acid remarks and Sharp had to withstand a fair amount of ribbing from other quarters. Everything was now on the line. If he had backed a winner, his film would have considerable value. But if Jahangir lost, then it would have been largely a waste of time.

Early results were reassuring. Jahangir demolished Bryan Patterson of England for the loss of only three points. Mo Asran took a game off him but was then slapped down for his impudence. Dean Williams of Australia could only manage five points in a match which lasted less than half an hour. Gamal Awad pinched a game in the quarter-finals but was never a serious threat. Hiddy Jahan took on Jahangir in the semi-finals. Seated in the audience, Hunt must have become progressively more uncomfortable. One of the strong men of the circuit was kept under constant bombardment until he conceded defeat with a 9–3, 9–3, 9–3 score.

Jahangir had reached the final but hit a snag: he had hurt his shoulder. The injury was so painful that he could hardly lift his racket above his head: 'Obviously, I didn't want to tell anyone because rumours spread like wildfire, giving advantage to opponents. I was afraid to go to doctor for same reason.' He had managed to disguise the injury during the other games and had even emerged as slight favourite for the title but he was not a hundred per cent fit. Should he take a chance and hope that his shoulder held up? Or was the risk of losing another major final too big?

He decided to play. The final would be played on a day that marked the second anniversary of Torsam's death. That had to be more than coincidence. He was destined to play and should not pull out. The injury would not endanger his career. Once on court, he would forget all about it. Again, he remembered the example of his father. Roshan lost seven teeth in a match but did not give up. Khans played on.

Rahmat showed him a video recording of the British Open final to remind him of the mistakes he had made then. Jahangir had done far too much running around and he had shown a fatal impatience in the fourth game. This time it would be different. He was to keep Hunt on the move as much as possible and conserve his own energies by controlling the rallies. Time was on his side. The longer the match went, the more the odds swung in his favour. Hunt would be fearing another two-hour match. After the last one, he was in such bad shape that he was passing blood.

When the day of the final arrived, Rahmat went along to Jahangir's room to wake him up. They would all have breakfast together. Two-year old Natasha was wearing a sticking plaster on her chin – a legacy from playing about with her father's razor. She was proud of her injury and advertised it: Jahangir had to conceal his and hope that it went unnoticed. They took a taxi to the complex and went off to the little room that had been assigned to them. Jahangir changed into his kit and put on his track suit.

Geoff Hunt was in the adjoining dressing room trying to concentrate all his energies on what lay ahead. Jahangir had beaten him in Cologne but much more was at stake now. He had the champion's knack of pulling out all the stops when it really mattered. He was quietly confident that he could do it again.

Rahmat, meanwhile, gave last minute advice: 'You have been working for nearly two years. Very hard work, Jahangir, on court and off it. Time has come. Allah has given you another chance to complete your brother's mission. And for past two years we've been through lots of problems and hard work. Always remember Allah on court and off. Remember Allah with each stroke you play. Allah. Win or lose, that's his will. Your duty is to work hard and see what happens.'

Fired by these words, Jahangir went out on court to rapturous applause. This was no partisan audience in Bromley. They were ready to cheer both players. When the first game began, Jahangir did far more boasting than in his earlier marathons. He took Hunt up and back time and again. Hunt responded by striking the ball higher on the front wall and even lobbing at times. Rahmat was alarmed that this might expose the weakness in Jahangir's shoulder but it held up. His adrenalin was pumping and he felt no pain.

The first game lasted well over fifty minutes. Jahangir lost it but was not at all upset: 'I felt I could outlast him. I could see Geoff was starting to get tired and I knew that my strategy had worked.' There was another encouraging sign. At the end of the game, Hunt argued with the officials. That was not his style at all. Jahangir was evidently getting to him. When Hunt shouted at a refereeing decision in the second game, Rahmat smiled across at Jahangir. They had got him on the run. His famed self-control was cracking around the edges. Jahangir followed the same strategy in the second and third games, winning both 9–2. Before the fourth game, Rahmat reminded him that, if he won, they would take the trophy back to Torsam's grave. It was just the inspiration he needed. Hunt had now shot his bolt. Occasional flashes of magic came from his racket but he could muster no serious opposition. The game, match and championship went to Jahangir Khan.

Rahmat rushed on court and the two of them – in a quite unrehearsed gesture of thanks – got down on their knees and paid homage to Allah. Jahangir was seventeen and he was World Champion.

The tumult of the celebrations carried him along but his mind was never far from the promise he had made to his brother. Two years to get to the very top; he had made it with only hours to spare. Though he enjoyed the fruits of victory, the finest moment was yet to come. They flew back to Karachi with the trophy and took it to the grave of Torsam Khan.

'Oh, Allah, forgive us. Our living and our dead, those that are present and those that are absent, our young and our old, our men and our women. Oh, Allah, those of us to whom you give life, keep firm in the faith . . . Truly, to you do we all belong and to you we must return. Amen.'

142

UNSQUASHABLE

Jahangir was the toast of Pakistan. A country with a turbulent history and some colossal problems had something to shout about at last. He returned home to the kind of welcome which had greeted Hashim Khan forty years earlier. Now as then, thousands of people who had no real idea what the game of squash was, turned out to acclaim him. There would be official receptions and banquets in his honour but his first priority was to spend time with his family. He had once again connected them with the world title. After a gap of almost twenty years, the Khan dynasty could exert its polite tyranny over the rest of the world's squash-players once more.

It was just like old times but in one respect totally different from them. The pride, the joy, the shared enthusiasm were the same but the rewards were much greater. During a long and successful career as a player, Roshan Khan made no substantial money out of the game. He returned to his old house and his old job. Jahangir was a child of the squash boom. World champions attracted lucrative advertising contracts and large fees for exhibition games. One of the first things he did when he had enough money was to have a new family home built in the exclusive Defence area of the city. Roshan Khan would no longer have to be afraid to invite friends to his home in case he let his country down.

Jahangir was not only in Karachi to receive congratulations. He took part in the Pakistan Masters and gave his countrymen the thrill of seeing their own world champion about his business. Hiddy Jahan held him up for a while in the semi-final. Maqsood Ahmed fought hard before being swept aside in the final. The conqueror of the world exuded confidence.

143

Everyone was starting to see his aura now. He was young enough to stay at the top for many years. The Barrington era had faded. The Hunt era looked as if it has just been brought to an end. The new Khan era had dawned.

Rahmat received his share of the congratulations. His role had been crucial from start to finish. Nur Khan was amongst the first to admit that sending Jahangir to Britain had been the correct decision. He had set Rahmat a time limit of three years and told him that he was accountable to the nation. Carrying his responsibility lightly, Rahmat had helped Jahangir to achieve his goal in a year less than was stipulated. It was a coaching triumph. Roshan felt vindicated as well. It had fallen to him to give the casting vote and he had been under severe pressure to keep his son in Pakistan. All kinds of blandishments had been offered to Jahangir if he stayed, even a house with servants. He preferred a small flat in Wembley, which he shared with his cousin's family and with an ever-present film cameraman.

Stuart Sharp was elated. He had realised that the triumph in Toronto was not the end of his film. It was just one climactic moment which would be succeeded by many more, each one of greater import because of their cumulative effect. A first world title was an achievement but supposing he equalled Hunt's record of four? Or beat it with five? Then there was Jahangir's avowed aim to reclaim the British Open record for his family. That meant he had to win *nine* titles. The story could run and run. Sharp made a mental note to order some more cans of film.

When the new year came, Jahangir launched himself with a win over Hiddy Jahan in the Irish Open. In the Lookers Masters Tournament, he beat Gawain Briars and in the ISPA Smirnoff Masters – scene of the previous year's upset – he downed Roland Watson. His most emphatic tournament win ever came in the final of Thorntons ISPA Championship. He extinguished the luckless Maqsood Ahmed 9–0, 9–0, 9–0. This ominous scoreline, which made Jahangir the first player ever to win an international tournament without dropping a point, was posted against a player who had beaten Hunt in the final of the 1981 Swiss Masters and who had won the individual event of the ISRF World Championship in 1977 when he defeated his brother Mohamed Saleem.

The word went out. Nobody was safe. Reputations meant nothing to Jahangir. He cut them to ribbons with an Unsquashable racket. At the McEwans Lager Open Championship in Stockton in March, he accounted for five of the most famous names in the game – Mo Yasin, Mohibullah junior, Gamal Awad, Qamar Zaman and Hiddy Jahan. The Patrick International Squash Festival at Chichester offered a faint chance of a hiccup in his progress but it was not to be. When he met Geoff Hunt in the final again, there was no marathon slugging contest. Hunt bowed out 9–2, 9–2, 9–6.

The Audi British Open was held at Bromley once more and it was felt that only Hunt had any hope of checking Jahangir's forced march through the record books. Sadly, he was found to be suffering from a cracked vertebrae which made him withdraw from the event. His injury was compounded by arthritic problems in the back and hip. A groan of disappointment went around the sport when he reluctantly announced his retirement. His era had been a fine one and his name would remain bright.

Deprived of his main opposition, Jahangir went through the tournament without dropping a game. After removing Mohibullah, Alauddin, Norman and Zaman, he got involved in yet another sophisticated brawl with Hiddy Jahan. Always a hardy opponent, Jahan made him earn his victory. Stuart Sharp feels that he himself deserved a Survival Award for filming this match. Jahan took exception to his presence and stormed off court to berate him at one point. Those dark Pathan eyes were feared by referees around the world. When they blazed with anger, they could fry an egg at fifty paces. Sharp got the full laser treatment without benefit of anaesthetic. His beard was singed for weeks.

Foreign travels beckoned. Jahangir scooped up the Bavarian Open in Munich then changed his marks into francs en route to winning the Siporex French Open in Paris. With another season over, he could return to Pakistan for a brief holiday.

What they admired about him back home was his genuine modesty. It was hardly a family trait. Torsam had been a superb player and he was ready to shout about it from the rooftops. Jahangir was more reticent. Those years as the delicate boy at the end of the queue had left their mark. With all his triumphs, he remained humble. When he went to practise at the Fleet Club with his father, there was no standing on ceremony. He was as approachable as before and he would oblige anyone who asked for a game. The officers at the club were honoured to have a hit with a reigning world champion, all the more so because he gave his time freely in the spirit of friendship.

Rahmat had been quick to exploit Jahangir's name. His cousin joined the board of Unsquashable and endorsed its range of rackets and sportswear. Another company had been set up as well. Jahangir Khan Enterprises, based in Toronto, was more wide-ranging in its activities. The wholesome image that he projected was ideal for marketing and promoting certain products. Young, fit, single, clean-cut, glowing with health, he was the ad man's dream. His name could command fees that ran into thousands. At his own insistence, the only products he endorsed had to be healthy. Tobacco, drink or other harmful substances were on the prohibited list.

Those who had the gall to criticise Rahmat's handling of his player might have been less keen to take on Jahangir himself if they had to do so without payment. Rahmat did not take a penny from him in coaching fees: 'Jahangir is family. I could never ask him to pay for coaching. He stayed with us as my cousin. Naturally, I will take my percentage from the management of Jahangir Khan but he knows that my coaching comes free. Always.'

Jahangir's comment is instructive: 'Rahmat and me, we both can share everything. Like we lose something, we share it, we win something, we'll share it. You cannot get closer than that.' When he lost the final of the 1981 British Open, it was Rahmat who comforted him and shielded him from the media. Whenever someone asked why he had lost, Rahmat would be there to answer that they had put the defeat behind them. He was much more than just a coach. Knowing that he himself could never reach the pinnacle of the sport, he gave up his career to invest time and energy and emotional capital in

Jahangir. Their partnership went deeper than a normal coach-player relationship. They were engaged in a spiritual quest together. They fought their way to the top with an endearing mixture of grim determination and boyish fun.

There was a new departure for the phenomenon in 1982: American hardball squash. Hashim, Azam, Roshan and Mohibullah senior had mastered the game. So had Hashim's sons. It was Jahangir's turn to play the alternative version. It was not a simple transition. There was more than just a harder ball, a lower tin and a different scoring system to accommodate. Jahangir had to learn to think and move faster, to hit lower and with more punch, to snap up his wrist action and to shorten his backswing. He soon discovered that the ball does not die so easily. It was more difficult to hit outright winners in America.

He was also reminded of what it was like to lose. Both Mario Sanchez, the stylish Mexican, and Mark Talbott, the lean Floridian, beat him at their own game. But he had seen enough to want to try harder. He would be back to America when his other commitments would allow. In deference to American protests, he accepted that he could not really claim to be *world* champion of squash until he was king of both games. Other members of the Khan dynasty had been double champions. He resolved to follow in their footsteps.

Australia now called him. He flew to Queensland to win the Brisbane Open then stopped off at Sydney to beat Dean Williams in the final of the Sun Alliance Australian Men's Championship. Moving on to New Zealand, he played and won four tournaments on the trot, quenching the urgent flame of Gamal Awad in the first three finals. His trip down under had been an unqualified success but it was never to be his favourite part of the world. He was given a good welcome and the press gave the game reasonable coverage, but jet lag was always a problem, not to mention the associations with Torsam that Australia held.

Back in England once more, he went up to another place that had links with his brother: Leicester. In the final of the ICI Perspex World Masters, he flattened the hapless Gamal Awad once more. Then came the big event, the defence of his world title in Birmingham. It was a cold November in the Midlands but he warmed up his opponents with some attacking squash. England's Richard Mosley and Andy Dwyer managed only two points apiece against him, Ali Aziz of Egypt upped the bidding to three before Phil Kenyon came in with a respectable fifteen. Glenn Brumby fared less well in the semi-final, gaining just three miserable points. Dean Williams, the bouncy and idiosyncratic Australian, actually took a game off him in the final but it did not affect the result.

Jahangir Khan was conqueror of the world. Again. He brought his tournament year to a close with a victory over Zaman in the final of the Swiss Masters. He was not only unbeatable, he was beginning to be unapproachable on court. The distance he put between himself and his rivals seemed to widen all the time. The man was unsquashable. It soon became clear to the others that the only way to beat Jahangir Khan was to challenge him to a game of Trivial Pursuit.

How did he maintain his dominance over the others? Is it possible to plumb his secret or does it lie in some mystic realm? Jahangir himself hides nothing: 'If you are fit enough, then obviously you can reach the ball, and if you have good control, then obviously you can put ball away from your partner.' Islam was central to his whole approach: 'I learn lot of discipline from my religion. Not to drink any alcohol, not to do many other things. In our religion, there are so many things which help sportsmen, I would say. I have seen many players, I mean, they want to become a world champion as well, and they want to enjoy their laugh, which is they want to have late nights and go to disco. It's just not possible, I would say.'

To squash the unsquashable, you have to be as fit and as wholly dedicated to his craft as Jahangir is. It is a tall order for any player. Only people like Barrington and Hunt managed to turn physical conditioning into an art. Nobody currently in the game was able to stand the pace that Jahangir was setting. Then there was his flexibility: 'I can play two types of game. I can play long game for one or two hours and I can play stroke game which is short game. I mean, when I get a chance, play a winner. So I depend on two games. But some players, they are not fit enough. Always play short game. But one day, it's not working, the same shot, they are in trouble.'

Jahangir summed up his art in a sentence: 'I work hard, I live a physical life and I have ambition and that makes me a winner.' Stated with such disarming modesty, it all sounds so simple. But the statistics of the year 1982 reveal a trail of devastation. He swept through the sport like a hurricane. Those who had prophesied that it would take him five years to make it were left with egg on their faces. Jahangir Khan was the future of squash for a very long time.

The world champion did all he could to foster his sport and to consolidate his dominance of it but the game was to be blemished in 1982. On 15 July, Mohibullah Khan junior and a friend, Hidayatullah, were arrested by British customs officers at Heathrow Airport. A million dollars' worth of heroin was found concealed in their suitcase. Mairaj Husain, Chairman of Pakistan's Narcotics Control Board, was scandalised: 'This took us by storm. We did not know what heroin was when this happened. It is still called *charas* like opium.' Mohibullah protested his innocence, claiming that he did not put the drug into his suitcase, but he was tried and found guilty nevertheless. Both men began long prison sentences.

The case rocked the squash community. Many of its Pakistani members – friends of Mohibullah – were contacted by the police to answer questions about him. The player not only ended his squash career in a miserable way, he caused eruptions back in Pakistan. To bring dishonour on one's family and tribe was a grave offence. There was much shame and embarrassment in Peshawar. One of Mohibullah's brothers took it particularly hard: twelve-year old Jansher Khan. He could not believe that his brother was guilty. He felt the urge to help Mohibullah in the only way he knew – on a squash court.

It would take years before Jansher was ready to enter the senior arena but his mind was fixed on it. He and Jahangir had something in common. Brothers who, in their different ways, acted as a spur and gave them a mission. Family ties are unbreakable in the Pathan culture. Bonds between brothers are especially strong. Jahangir drew strength from Torsam; Jansher, in time, would gain some of his inspiration from his own elder brother.

When the New Year began, the first item on the agenda was

149

the Pakistan Open which was played at the PIA Complex in Karachi. Like most of the leading professionals, Jahangir was sponsored by PIA. Since he was thus 'serving' in the air force, he received the salary appropriate to his rank. That rank would improve as he continued to conquer new heights. PIA were generous with their staff and Jahangir was allowed free travel on their aircraft to any part of the world, a tremendous bonus in his line of work. His father, Roshan, had had to beg the Pakistan Navy for the price of a ticket to London.

Jahangir's fame and fortune not only enabled him to have the new home built near Clifton Beach, but also turned the spotlight back on Roshan who was sadly neglected by his countrymen. He had been living in the shadows for many years until his two sons became professional squash players. The father of a world champion was a VIP but much more use could have been made of his coaching talents in the previous decade. He had been involved in some national junior coaching schemes in the 1960s but had then been largely forgotten. His son's eminence now gained him his rightful share of respect and attention.

Although Jahangir helped to pay for the home, his father was the head of it. Even a luminary like Jahangir had to show respect to his elders. He could arrive back home with an armful of trophies but, if his father told him to wash the car, that is what he would do. The house itself is a fine, big dwelling on a spacious plot of land. Two crossed squash rackets are painted high up on the side wall. The plaque at the front of the house is an example of Pathan pride. It bears the legend 'Champions Villa 1957 1981'. Crossed squash rackets again make an eye-catching design and there is some leafwork beneath the dates that mark the triumphs of father and son.

The house is worlds away from the mud dwelling in Nawakille where Roshan and Nasrullah were born, or from the little place in Abbysinia Lines where Jahangir was brought up. They have moved across the city and up in the social scale. As is usual, they employ a Pathan youth to sit outside the gates of the house to guard it. During cold nights, he will light a fire by the roadside like his compatriots nearby. In this way, the old and the new happily coexist.

In the final of the Pakistan Open, Hiddy Jahan took another crack at the champion. Even his power and deftness and agile squash brain could not do more than take a game from Jahangir. Roshan was pleased to see Jahan. They had first met in the 1960s when Jahan was supposed to attend some national junior trials. On the slow, six hundred mile journey from Quetta to Karachi, Jahan was seriously injured when hit by a signal. Anyone hearing this famous story for the first time usually enquires with solicitude about the signal. Jahan is a big man.

Taken to hospital, he discharged himself and raced to take part in the trials. When Roshan saw the bandaged figure coming on court, he could not believe his eyes. Not unnaturally, Jahan failed to do justice to himself in the trials. He went back to Quetta and spent three months or more in hospital. Extensive injuries were revealed. But it had not stopped him playing squash. The story says a lot about Jahan's bravery and gives an insight into the Pathan mentality.

Rahmat and Jahangir decided to be more selective about his tournaments in 1983. If he did not play in so many, it gave others a chance to win. Again, some of the smaller ones were a distraction from the main business of retaining his major titles. There was another calculation involved in the programming. Jahangir's management was asking for appearance money from some organisers. The world champion's presence at a tournament gives it status, guarantees publicity and attracts sponsors. Critics take a jaundiced view of it all but Rahmat Khan has another explanation: 'We don't call it appearance money. It's a fee for Jahangir's services. Organisers can use him to get sponsors interested. Jahangir will wear their logo on his shirt. If organisers do their job properly, they can make a profit out of the system.'

One tournament that could not be left off the list was the Patrick International at Chichester which evoked memories of the epic battle with Hunt in 1981 and sadder memories of the depleted former champion in the 1982 event. Nobody was allowed to dwell on the past for long for this was the final in which Gamal Awad elected himself as the person to grind Jahangir Khan into the floor. In the course of this longest-ever

151

match, the Egyptian must have covered miles and expended masses of energy but it did not bring the desired result. Beaten to a frazzle, Awad limped off court with ashen face. Jahangir Khan really did seem invincible.

At the ensuing British Open, the Egyptian's challenge crumbled early in the final and Jahangir took his second title. Two down, seven to go. Was it really possible to replace Geoff Hunt's name in the record books? Hashim Khan thought so – and he had just seen Jahangir lose at Bromley in 1981. As he presented the trophies, he issued a warning: 'I think he's the best for his age in the world these days. And I tell you one thing, if Jahangir start to win British Open, any time he start to win, he will be winner more than eight times for sure.' Family pride or a realistic prediction? It remains to be seen.

Jahangir went on to mop up whatever he wanted – the Mennen Cup in Toronto, the French Open, the Malaysian Open, the World Individual Championship in New Zealand and so on. Autumn found him in the unlikely setting of Warrington where he won the World Masters title for the second time with a 3–1 victory over Zaman. Jahangir was in reflective mood: 'I know that I will lose one day. I don't mind to lose in the future. It's good for me. And then I can work harder and harder. I can come back again.' They would be prophetic words.

That same month, Jahangir flew to America and won the Boston Open by beating the top-ranked Mark Talbott. Then it was back to Europe again for the Canadian Club World Open in Munich. In his second defence of his title, Jahangir met some familiar faces along the way – Ahmed Safwat, Phil Kenyon, Gamal Awad. The final set him up against Chris Dittmar of Australia, a big, powerful young man with the fluid movement of a boxer. It was the first time that two teenagers had contested the world title. Dittmar was outclassed and went down 9–3, 9–6, 9–0. Three world titles – only one more needed to draw level with Hunt.

The Fleischman World Professional Championship was held in Toronto, the city where Jahangir had fulfilled his promise to his brother. It provided him with some more happy memories. He beat Mark Talbott again to take another world title. Nobody could deny his supremacy. He was top of the heap in the softball and hardball variations of squash. A relative newcomer to hardball, he had quelled the acknowledged master of the sport. Soft or hard, he was still unsquashable.

Rahmat Khan was actively engaged in everything that his player did. Just because he was champion, he did not get released from onerous training sessions. Indeed, it was even more important to maintain his high level of fitness now. The demands upon him were greater. Coach and player also developed their off court activities. Jahangir Khan Enterprises was flourishing. Unsquashable was starting to sponsor a small amateur tournament in the London area. It would also sponsor a tournament in Scandinavia in time.

To the outward eye, everything appeared to be running smoothly. Rahmat's detractors were saying that all he had to do was to sit back and wait for the money to roll in. This was not true at all. Apart from his coaching commitments with Jahangir, he played regular exhibition matches against him all over the world. He also held coaching clinics. On the road for several weeks at a time, he was torn away from his family. This put a heavy strain on the marriage but it was more than strong enough to survive. Josie Khan had the right temperament to cope with the problems of being the wife of a travelling squash professional. And there was always the telephone.

Rahmat's business ventures did not always meet with success. Unsquashable went through a very rocky period. There were difficulties with distribution and management problems at the British end of the enterprise. Things were so bleak at one point that Rahmat thought he might lose his house – they had moved to Croxley Green now. But he prayed and he worked and he hung in there. When some management changes were made, the business picked up immediately and continued on an upward curve. Another crisis had been averted.

But it was the squash itself that Rahmat and Jahangir loved the most. They were never tired of working on the latter's game, keeping it up to scratch, extending it, refining it, varying it. Jahangir could beat anyone in the world but he still wanted to play better squash. Expressed modestly, his ambitions nonetheless were astounding: five world titles; nine British Opens; an unbeaten record that went on indefinitely. Could any human being attain those goals?

Jahangir Khan did and could. The opponents kept on coming and he kept on knocking them over. He floated through the years on a magic carpet of excellence. Sometimes it would soar to the heavens. Other times it would dip low but it was always out of reach of the others. He was above his peers and they could not find a way to rise to his level.

The major titles came in a steady flow – World Opens, British Opens, Masters Tournaments, National Opens, World Team Events. He kept on winning because it was that important to him. People feted him wherever he went. Heads of state wanted to meet him. Showbiz and sporting celebrities flocked to befriend him. Television companies made documentaries about him. Publishers sought instructional books from him. It was a ceaseless routine of hard work and travel.

He loved it: 'I wanted every tournament in the world. I just want to keep carrying on because I'm young and let's see how long I can keep carrying on with that. I still work hard as I was doing before and I know that many players are coming up, young players, and I know that one day I will be beaten. But I just want to carry on as long as I can go.'

He was to go on for five and a half glorious years. Until November 1986.

LOSING AND WINNING

Ross Norman was the absolute antithesis of Jahangir Khan. The tall, spare, blond New Zealander was a man who liked to plough a lonely furrow. He did not rely on a coach or a manager. He did his own training and programming. He was not a showy player, just an immensely capable one. Norman was the professionals' professional. The man admired by his peers for his honesty, fairness, competitiveness, racket work and willingness to suffer. He was a natural athlete of the type who would excel at any sport. A perfect all-rounder with an outstanding all-round game: thorough, efficient, controlled, sound in technique. A parachuting accident all but crippled him in the summer of 1983. His career in squash seemed to be over.

But it was just the kind of challenge on which he thrived. Unable to walk for months and out of the game for much longer, he showed guts and single-mindedness in fighting back. His damaged knee slowly improved. He had to rebuild muscle, regain fitness, work on his mental toughness, re-discover his racket skills. It was a long, wearying process but he was not deterred. He set himself the target of toppling Jahangir Khan, on his own, however long it took. And he made no secret of the fact. When he was able to compete again, he warned the world champion that he would beat him one day. Jahangir would smile quietly. They all said that. But Norman was different. When he was knocked down, he got up and hit back harder.

Players knew him for his professionalism. Referees feared him for his stubbornness. He believed in fighting for his rights on court. If Jahangir got a bad call, he might treat the referee to a slow stare but that was all. He rarely spoke. Norman rarely stopped speaking if he thought he was getting a raw deal; nothing abusive, just a firm assertion of his point of view. It made for some interesting dialogues. Slight of build and with no superfluous body weight, he is as hard as iron in body and mind. Indeed, that is his nickname – the Iron Man.

His relentless pursuit of Jahangir began in 1984 when he was able to get back in the action again. As the months went by, he emerged as the front-runner to catch the world champion. If Jahangir did not take part in a tournament, Norman usually won it. If they met on court, Jahangir always won. The record had a definite pattern.

March	1984	FRENCH OPEN	semi-final	0–3
April	1984	BRITISH OPEN	quarter-final	0–3
December	1984	WORLD OPEN	semi-final	0–3
December	1984	AL FALAJ	final	0–3
October	1985	US OPEN	final	0–3
October	1985	CANADIAN OPEN	final	0–3
November	1985	SWISS MASTERS	final	0–3
December	1985	WORLD OPEN	final	1–3
December	1985	WORLD TEAM C'SHIP	final	0–3
December	1985	AL FALAJ OPEN	final	0–3
February	1986	ICI OPEN	final	0–3
February	1986	SPANISH OPEN	final	0–3
April	1986	BRITISH OPEN	final	0–3

Only one game was yielded by Jahangir in thirteen meetings and yet Norman's hopes were never dashed. That one game had been in the World Open in Cairo. Jahangir had been below form. He was troubled by a stomach bug, affected by an injury, unhappy with the court. He asserted himself to win but Norman had pushed him hard enough to wrest a game from him. It could be done. If a player could stay on court with the world champion long enough, they could beat him. Norman schemed on doing just that.

He trained, he planned, he watched Jahangir in action. His next opportunity did not come until the final of the World Open in Toulouse. They were in the glare of a·global spotlight.

It was the most propitious time to take his amazing record away from him.

When Jahangir Khan came out on court at the Palais des Sports, he was given a thunderous round of applause by thousands of excitable French spectators. Ross Norman got a warm welcome as well. It was as if the crowd sensed that something sensational was going to happen. They were as keyed up as the players. Jahangir was not at his best. He had thickened slightly around the waist. He was short of match practice. Chris Dittmar had given him a torrid time in the semi-final before he was beaten. There was another telling factor: Rahmat was absent. His wife had been taken ill and he was at her bedside. There would be no secret signals during a game, no advice in the rest period. Jahangir was on his own.

As soon as the game started, he had trouble with the Merco ball on which stripes had been painted so that the television cameras could pick it up. The players were used to the sunken reflective spot technique used on the Dunlop Teleball. Whenever one of the painted stripes hit the floor, the ball would skid then bounce up at an unpredictable angle. The problem was the same for both players but it somehow unsettled Jahangir the more. He was having difficulty seeing the Merco ball.

Norman took the first game in just under half an hour by dint of superior concentration. He adapted to the conditions better. His problem was with the referee, John Robinson, whose decisions he queried more than once. At one point in the second game, he came off court to argue with the referee. Jahangir was given valuable recovery time but it did not seem to help him. He lost the second game in just under three-quarters of an hour.

Shah Jahan, brother of Hiddy and a France-based professional, came over to Jahangir during the break and asked him what was wrong. Jahangir shrugged. He did not know. But he just did not feel like playing. His motivation, his lust for success had somehow let him down. Even though he was just two games down, most people did not foresee his removal. He would come back and win a five-game thriller. The Eiffel Tower would fall before Jahangir Khan did.

Their optimism was not shared by the player himself who

was feeling tired, jaded and curiously uninterested. Jahangir then summoned up his energies and gave a passable impersonation of his old self. Hitting the ball more crisply and with greater confidence, he staged a recovery to win 7–9. Like the spectators, Norman expected the fightback to continue. Jahangir was at his best when his back was to the wall. Yet somehow the fireworks did not happen. Norman suddenly found himself 8–1 up and on the brink of a historic victory. When he took the championship point, the audience went wild.

The conqueror of the world had finally been conquered himself. Norman whooped with delight: 'It was an amazing feeling. I could just let go and shout for joy. I had done it the hard way, worn him off the court, the greatest player this game has ever seen.'

While Ross basked in his acclaim, Jahangir sat ruefully in his seat. He took his defeat well and made no excuses for it. Ross Norman got it together at the right time. He had been outplayed. Some people rushed to write the Pakistani off. They said that he had lost his appetite for the game; that his era had come to an end; that he had been so far ahead of his rivals, it made him complacent. He had slackened off and this was the result.

Jahangir took all the criticism on the chin. He also took his revenge at the first available opportunity. Norman was crushed mercilessly this time and in all their subsequent meetings. Jahangir seemed anxious to prove that the win had been a flash in the pan. But another shock was in store for him in the new year. He got to the final of the Spanish Open in March and found himself facing Jansher Khan, seventeen-year old brother of Mohibullah junior. Tall, thin and wiry, Jansher looked like a human windmill when his right arm described swishing half-circles. He retrieved magnificently and covered the court easily with his loping stride. Jahangir beat him but had to surrender a game to his fellow-countryman.

Hiddy Jahan spotted the danger at once: 'Jahangir should have slapped him down then when he had the chance. If you let him get into the game, you're in trouble.' Jahan's tip was an accurate one. To the surprise of everyone, Jansher Khan got to the final of the 1987 British Open, beating players like Norman, Dittmar and Briars along the way. These matches had tested him and Jahangir was able to beat him in straight games but Jansher was certainly a player of the future. He would need to be watched carefully.

Trouble first came from another direction. When Jahangir played in Sydney that summer, he was defeated by Rodney Martin. The possessor of the longest legs in squash, Martin is also a beautiful shot-maker with the courage to go for his shots. Young, strong and daring, he sent the home crowd into ecstasies with his win over the deposed world champion. Was Jahangir really nearing the end of his days at the top?

When the World Championships came in sight, more than one squash journalist wondered if Jahangir would be unable to regain his crown. Something had happened to him. He was not the same. Rahmat knew this. Privately, he was having doubts about the World Open. He had not spent so much time with Jahangir in the previous year. Now that the Jahangir Khan Roadshow was running, it carried itself along. Rahmat only came into action to help during the major tournaments.

Niggling injuries had troubled the player against Norman and Martin. There was also a question mark over his weight and fitness. Again, he had become engaged to a girl in Pakistan and had been travelling to and fro at every opportunity. When the engagement was broken off, there was bound to be some emotional disturbance. But he was still the finest squash player of his generation. All he needed was conditioning.

Rahmat went with him to the Cathay Pacific Dunlop Open in Hong Kong. Coached by Mo Yasin, Jansher was full of fight and supremely fit. The audience saw something they would not have believed possible. JK Mark I was beaten by JK Mark II in straight games! Before the shock had worn off, Jansher beat him again in the Pakistan Open. Eyes popped at the 3–2 scoreline. Jahangir had looked far from fit. What of his chances in the World Open?

They, too, were scuppered by Jansher. In a tense semi-final that could have gone either way, Jansher secured the crucial advantage and won 3–1. It was becoming a habit. Two more defeats followed – in the US Open and the Swiss Open. In both matches, Jahangir came very close to winning and played superlative squash. But Jansher kept winning.

His sixth victory came in the final of the PIA Masters in Karachi, an extraordinary affair because the partisan crowd actually booed Jansher Khan, their home-grown world champion. Lifted by the vocal support, Jahangir came from behind to make it 2–2 but his challenge weakened in the fifth game. Six of the best for Jansher!

A seventh win was gained in a luxury hotel in Muscat at the Al Falaj Open. Jahangir was disgusted with how badly he played on that occasion. Going back to Pakistan, he trained madly. He was in much better condition in January 1988 for the Daily Mail Jersey International. Ross Norman scored four points in the first game and that was it. Showing all his old authority, Jahangir wiped out his opponent without compunction.

Just when he was getting back into his stride, Jahangir met and lost to Jansher again the Spanish Open. He went on to Paris for the Guy Laroche French Open. The lower tin and the experimental scoring system were being used and most of the players seemed to favour the changes. Jahangir was one of them, coasting through to the final to the inevitable confrontation with Jansher.

The world champion was in confident mood. He had played well in the previous round and enjoyed a lot of media attention. Jahangir waited quietly like a greyhound in the slips. When the game started, he was off. Jansher's rich abilities as a retriever were put to the test as Jahangir sent him racing all over the court. The younger player came back strongly but it was Jahangir's game 15–9. Jansher was upset by the reverse and tightened his game to win 10–15 in the second. Then it was Jahangir's turn to take charge. In an always nerve-racking third game, he finally came out on top 15–13.

It was not the first time he had had a two game advantage over the stick-like Jansher but he had never pressed it home before. This time it was different. When Jansher struggled, he contained his man and won the last game 15–5. It was a more decisive win than the score suggests and Jahangir was on air. Jansher, by contrast, was in tears, having been humbled by his rival at last.

The British Open now became the focus of attention. Could Jahangir actually win his seventh title in a row? His performance in France had heartened his supporters but there was one last tournament before all roads led to Wembley. It was in Monte Carlo. Returning from Pakistan, Jansher inflicted yet another narrow victory on Jahangir and signalled that he was on hand to relieve him of his British Open title as well. Jansher was cockily confident – 'I will beat Jahangir'. The older player was cautiously optimistic – 'I think I can win'.

In the event, it was Jansher who got beaten. He fell in his semi-final to the vivacious strokeplay of Rodney Martin. Jahangir had a 3–1 win over Dittmar to book his place in the final. Wembley Conference Centre was packed to the rafters. Tension was high. Speculation was rife. It was the fiftieth anniversary of the greatest squash championship of them all. Hashim Khan had come over from America to be in the audience. Could Jahangir equal his seven titles or would the lanky Australian get the better of him as well?

While the players knocked up, Jonah Barrington was asked to comment on the possible result. He forecast a fascinating duel between two opposing styles. He also made the point that it must be wonderful to play an Open Championship final in front of such a huge audience instead of – as in his day – one man and a dog. He was overstating his case but the point was taken. In the years since he had sweated blood to bring home the bacon for his country squash had seen profound changes. The final was now played inside a glorified fish tank.

Caution marked the early exchanges. Ten minutes passed before a point was scored. First blood to Jahangir. He established a short lead then there was a dispute over his ball. A let was called but Jahangir ignored the call, walking instead to the other side of the court and awarding the point to Martin. It was a sporting gesture that drew warm applause. There were to be no more favours. Sitting on the game throughout, Jahangir edged to a 9–2 win.

Two eras coalesced as Martin came off court. The man in his corner was none other than Geoff Hunt, a veteran of many campaigns against Jahangir. The Pakistani had the advice of Rahmat backed up by that of Umar Daraz, the coach of the

National Team. The second game began slowly, then lit up with flashes of brilliance. With the lead changing to and fro at will, the tension was mounting. Martin hit the decisive shot to win 9–10 and cheers reverberated around the building. An upset was on the cards after all.

Rahmat did not mince his words. He told Jahangir that he had let the advantage slip away from him and that he had to restore it in the next game. Increased effort was needed. Martin would be lifted by his success in the previous game and he would come out with new energy coursing through him. Jahangir had to subdue him firmly. This was the key game. He had to fight for every point.

Jahangir responded to his coach's exhortations. Changing gear, he imposed himself on the game so completely that Martin did not even score a point. The wind had been taken out of him. He looked pale and gaunt as he came off court. Hunt worked hard in the interval, trying his best to draw something extra out of his player. Martin obliged with some delightful touches in the fourth but they were not enough. Jahangir moved inexorably towards his seventh consecutive British Open title and sealed it with a stupendous kill in the left hand nick. All that Martin had to show for his efforts was one point.

It had been an intriguing final with fluctuating fortunes but there was no doubt that the stronger and more resourceful man came through in the end. He had confounded his critics and produced a performance that was vintage Jahangir Khan. The fish tank was his domain. He was a killer shark who cruised around with a jagged smile of confidence. Just when his opponent thought it was safe to go back in the water, Jahangir moved in to devour him with razor-sharp bites.

The media converged on the court. The new champion was interviewed by BBC Television and he made some gracious remarks about the luckless Martin. Photographers besieged him for a long time. When he was finally allowed off court, he walked straight over to the beaming Hashim Khan. They shook hands and embraced. One more link in the chain had been forged.

The Khan dynasty was supreme again. Fifty Open

Championships had been held and the Khans had now won twenty of them, with Nasrullah having at least a say in a further six. Jahangir's declared intent is to press on to the record of nine titles. With history at his elbow, who will be able to deny him?

Jahangir's momentous achievement could not have been more well-deserved. He had worked exceptionally hard to get himself somewhere near peak fitness. He had been through a long period of crisis and weathered it with extreme fortitude. A seventh title was a fitting reward for his impressive comeback.

'I know I will lose one day . . . I can come back again.'

His own words had been prophetic. He had held on to the title that meant most to him and he had done so with Rahmat's guidance. The duo had done it once more. But their season was not quite over. There was something else on Jahangir's shopping list.

The World Open title.

THE HIGHEST BOUNTY

A week is a long time in professional squash circles. Reputations can be made or lost. Psychological damage can be repaired or increased. Improvement can be sustained or sabotaged. Fears can be put to flight. Nerves can run amok. Ambitions can be fulfilled or ruined. Spirits can soar or be dashed. Rumours can exert a powerful influence. Attitudes can be revolutionised. The patient grind of a whole season can be celebrated or squandered.

Jahangir Khan arrived in Amsterdam for the 1988 NCM World Open, trailing clouds of glory. He was the new British Open champion. He had redeemed an otherwise disappointing season with a late flurry of brilliance. A week in Holland could easily take the shine off his revival. He was seeded to meet Jansher Khan in the final. It was not something he could approach with complete confidence. Out of their ten previous meetings, Jansher had won nine. Jahangir's only victory against his compatriot was in the French Open where the lower tin and experimental scoring system had been used.

Detractors and whisperers claimed that he would never have beaten Jansher in the British Open final. Rodney Martin, it was argued, did him a favour by removing his greatest obstacle. Martin and the equally talented Chris Dittmar could not impede Jansher this time. They were both in Jahangir's half of the draw. As the players gathered in the luxurious comfort of the Barbizon Palace Hotel, they knew that there would be gruelling times ahead. Jahangir and Jansher were set on another collision course. Neither of them would take kindly to anyone who tried to hinder their progress.

The event was held at the Rai-Amstelhal, a massive trade

centre to the south of the city. An all-glass court was mounted in one of the hanger-like exhibition halls. It was bedecked with advertisements for the sponsors, surrounded by banked seating that could accommodate a few thousand spectators and fronted by a trade exhibition. Golf, pool and snooker were on display alongside squash. Toyota brought its full range of cars, including its new smaller 'Squash' model.

There were immediate problems with lighting on court. The huge windows that ran along the top of the building had not been completely blacked out. Shafts of sunlight came in to dazzle and disturb. Players sometimes had difficulty picking out the ball. Some of the evening matches had to be delayed slightly until the sun had dipped. It was perhaps the only major sporting event in history where 'good light stopped play'. The summery weather made for a warm and almost sultry atmosphere inside the building and this had its effect on the ball in the various matches. Another hazard was the smell of fried food which wafted in from the catering stalls nearby. In its first staging of a World Open, Amsterdam had its teething troubles.

An attractive young lady acted as mistress of ceremonies, introducing the players in Dutch and English with the fluency of a hostess at a Eurovision Song Contest. It made a change from the portly authority of Norman de Mesquita but his knowledge of the game and its players was missed. In the build-up to the matches, the sense of occasion was slightly diminished.

When battle commenced, most of the minor irritations vanished. Jansher – whose name means Soul of a Tiger and who trains, appropriately, at Stripes Club in Ealing – disposed of Hans Frieling, the Netherlands' top player, with the loss of only four points. Phil Kenyon only took one more point from him in the next round. In the quarter-finals, Chris Robertson, the chirpy Australian who is ranked sixth in the world, gave the Pakistani more of a test but he still bowed out in straight games. Jansher was looking businesslike.

Jahangir was similarly brisk with his opponents. Austin Adarraga from down under managed a mere three points and his compatriot, Ricki Hill, ranked in tenth position, could only collect four. The quarter-finals pitted Jahangir against his cousin, close friend and practice partner, Umar Hayat Khan. It was the usual lively encounter with the scoreline of 9–1, 9–1, 9–4 an unfair reflection of Umar Hayat's sterling endeavours. Jahangir was clearly on song.

Ross Norman beat the promising Del Harris to eliminate any British interest and to earn himself the dubious privilege of a semi-final place against Jansher. Chris Dittmar won a riveting cut-and-thrust match against his fellow-countrymen, Rodney Martin, to take his place in the frame against Jahangir. New Zealand against the Tiger. Australia versus the Conqueror. The all too familiar geography of the later stages of a World Open. Europe had once again been wiped from the globe.

Jansher exuded the confidence of a reigning champion. He had got over his shock defeat in the British Open and was relishing the chance to remind everyone that he was still the world's number one. Jahangir was more subdued and reflective. After a light training session in the morning, he rested in his room and watched cricket on television. Rahmat was in some discomfort because he was fasting during Ramadan. The heatwave outside only served to make his throat even drier. Sharing a room with Umar Hayat Khan, he lay on the bed in a track suit and took a cautiously optimistic view. Jahangir should win. Inshallah.

The first semi-final was delayed for half an hour until the sun stopped peeping down on the court. Ross Norman then won himself a lot of new admirers with a gutsy performance which kept the result in doubt for well over an hour. He attacked Jansher from the outset and raced to a 7–2 lead. The champion refused to panic and simply upped the tempo to snatch the game 7–9. Norman was restricted to two points in the second game but he mounted a sustained challenge in the third game to take it 9–7. Jansher was looking vulnerable. His superior stamina told in the fourth game and he won 3–9 but Norman had stretched him.

It was very late before Jahangir stepped on court and he knew that he, too, would be pushed hard. Chris Dittmar had Norman's amazing resilience. No matter how many times he was beaten by an opponent, he always went into the next game believing he could win. Big, strong and fearless, he would never submit to psychological intimidation. He had another plus factor – the presence of his wife. The beautiful Leanne Dittmar is not only the best-dressed woman on the circuit, she has added a new sense of responsibility to her husband's game. Gone is the hell-raiser who used to stay up until the small hours on nights before a major final. He has learned to focus all his attention on the job in hand.

Dittmar showed his quality by gliding to a 7–2 lead. Jahangir replied by increasing the pace of his volleying assaults to win 7–9. He contained the Australian's brilliance more completely in the second game which he took 4–9. Dittmar slowed as the fierce pace was maintained by Jahangir who conceded five points before wrapping up the match. It had been an impressive display against a fine opponent but it left the Pakistani rather jaded: 'I am the oldest player in the top ten.' This was not strictly true but he had certainly been up there longer than any of the others. Only twenty-four and he was starting to feel his age. He cast an envious eye at Jansher and the sweet bird of youth.

Jahangir was at his most reserved next morning. He breakfasted in the hotel cafe at ten o'clock and left for the Rai-Amstelhal an hour later. He was very quiet on the twenty-minute journey and only raised a gentle smile when it was pointed out to him that the official programme had described him as 'married in Spain'. Rahmat was in his usual affable mood, chatting happily all the way.

When they got to the centre, they stripped off their track suits and did stretching exercises on the floor for a few minutes. Jahangir then went on court to warm up the ball. He and Rahmat began their time-honoured routine, the coach feeding the player on both sides of the court so that he could practise his volleys, drop shots and boasts. They were at once relaxed and serious.

Jansher soon arrived with his coach, Mo Yasin. While the others speeded up their work, the newcomers began their stretching exercises. Jahangir and Rahmat finished their work-out and gave their rivals a cheery greeting. There was much hilarity over Yasin's claim to be fasting during Ramadan, especially as he had been seen wolfing a hearty breakfast at the hotel. The players exchanged friendly banter. It was hard to believe that the two of them would be at each other's throats that evening. There can be few sports where basic cameraderie overrides other considerations at such a key moment.

Jahangir returned to the Barbizon Palace to shower and rest. He was British Open champion but the advantage still lay with Jansher. Nine wins out of ten meetings is a powerful statistic. The manner of those wins stirred uneasy memories for Jahangir. He had often been well ahead, only to see his lead clawed back by the younger player. At their most recent final in the Monaco Open, Jahangir was two games to love up and leading in the third. Then an unseen hand seemed to grab him and hold him back. Jansher had a breathtaking run of twenty-one points to win yet another title from his compatriot.

Rahmat walked headlong into a serious problem back at the hotel. A discussion with business partners posed a threat to the Khan dynasty. It was one of the worst things that could have happened on the day of a World Open final. Jahangir was deeply implicated but his coach wisely kept all mention of the affair from him. Rahmat bravely hid his business worries behind a reassuring smile.

Better news came when he went to his room. As was his habit, he opened the Koran at random to find a text for the day. He could have chosen any of the one hundred and fourteen sura or chapters in the book. What met his gaze was: 'Such is the bounty of God which He bestows on whom He will. And God is the lord of the highest bounty.' When Rahmat was working on the commentary for Stuart Sharp's film, *The Conqueror*, he had sought the advice of a friend who was well-versed in the Koran. To begin the film, they had chosen the identical text. The highest bounty. It was a good omen.

A large crowd flocked to the Rai-Amstelhal that evening. Television cameras were manoeuvred into position. The first match on court was the play-off to decide third and fourth places. Ross Norman and Chris Dittmar came out to provide the perfect curtain-raiser to the main event. All the pressures were off them. They played wondrous, free-flowing, un-inhibited squash. Dittmar's reputation as a touch player is well-established but Norman showed that he, too, has a wide range of shots in his quiver. Those who accuse him of being too relentlessly neat and orthodox were made to eat their words. He contributed his share towards the most entertaining match of the whole championship. It was a thrilling advertisement for the game. Dittmar emerged as the winner with a 9–6, 9–5, 9–5 scoreline.

After a short interval, the final of the Netherlandsche Credietverzekering Maatschappij World Open Championship was announced. First to come out was Jahangir Khan who received a torrent of warm applause. One of the incredible side-effects of his defeats by Jansher was that spectators began to identify much more with him. A man who had only ever inspired awe and respect before was now earning sympathy. Jansher entered breezily to his ovation with Yasin carrying his rackets. Rahmat slipped on quietly from a corner to join Jahangir.

This was the crucial match of the season. The world's number one against the man he had supplanted. Which one really was the best? Jahangir had patently closed the gap between them but he was far from being the favourite. Rahmat's prediction had been realistic: 'I give him only fifty-fifty to win tonight.' Yasin was far more confident about his own man's chances. He was certain that Jansher would have the edge. The teenager had grown in stature as a player since he had become world champion the previous autumn.

Jahangir served first. He deliberately extended the opening rally to seven minutes and two hundred and twenty-four strokes. Whole games have been won with less time and effort. Patient ferocity was the order of the day. He kept Jansher pinned in the back corners of the court and resisted the temptation to go for a winner. The unrelieved pressure eventually paid off as Jansher put the ball out on the left-hand wall. Jahangir had won the first test of endurance and the crowd had been released from its unbearable tension.

The game continued in the same vein. Jahangir forced the pace and Jansher ran tirelessly to retrieve, his long arm snaking out to hit everything that came his way. But it was the older player who was taking the initiative and calling the tune.

Jansher was forced into more errors. When he found himself 6–2 down, he mustered all his energies to come back at Jahangir and actually drew level. It was the last time he would get that close. Playing with a youthful zest that was tempered by great experience, Jahangir forged on to take the first game 9–6 in just under forty minutes.

In the brief time it took his player to change his shirt and have a drink, Rahmat passed on his advice: 'The plan is working. Keep him at he back of the court. He is standing two or three feet behind the T. Give him the feeling you're not going for a short game. And *boast* more. He is not ready for boasts. His balance is not right.' Invigorated by his lead, Jahangir went back on court to continue where he had left off. Spurred on by his own coach, Jansher came out to try to neutralise his opponent's tactics.

But he was quite unable to do so. Jahangir had pole position and he never relinquished it. All that Jansher could do was to stay in his slipstream. Early on in the game, Jahangir had an uncharacteristic argument with the referee, Don Wilkie, when he felt he had been deprived of a stroke. He surged on to 4–1, weakened slightly, then found new reserves of energy. His boasts were putting Jansher in all kinds of trouble and the spectators were treated to the unusual sight of the world champion being bamboozled so completely that he was flat-footed. Jahangir won the game 9–2.

Rahmat was ready with a stern warning: 'Okay, Jahangir. You've done well. You're well ahead. But you've been in this position before. Don't throw away your advantage this time or it will haunt you for ever. Remember Monaco. You must push yourself even harder. You're tired, I know, but so is Jansher. He's been on court for almost an hour with nothing to show for it. You've got two games. Take the third. This must be the final one for you. Fight, Jahangir. *Fight!*'

Taking the advice to heart, the player went back on court to continue the war of attrition. He was helped by the fact that Jansher made no tactical changes. He was clearly hanging on in the belief that his man would tire as he had done in their earlier matches. When he reached 3–0, Jahangir recalled the final in Monaco. This time he would not crumble. Even though Jansher edged his way back to 3–2, Jahangir kept his nerve. After a long passage of defensive play, he took the next point with a delectable drop shot.

Boasts, reverse angles and lobs kept Jansher in frantic pursuit all round the court but he was chasing a lost dream. Jahangir was going for the post now. His last five points came with dazzling winners that drew explosive applause. Jansher Khan was in uncharted territory. He was in a world final against a Jahangir who was firing on all cylinders. The difference was in sheer class. The older man out-thought, out-hit and out-ran him at every turn. As Jahangir took the final crushing point with another flashing winner, he punched the air with pride and delight.

He was world champion again. The highest bounty was his.

Rahmat was first on court to embrace him. Jansher looked hurt and bemused. As the ovation echoed around the building, the Khan dynasty moved into a new dimension. Jahangir had restored its pride. His game had been a compendium of family strengths. He had Hashim's power, Azim's artistry, Roshan's magical touch and something of Mohibullah senior's audacity. Blended with his own unique qualities, it was an irresistible combination.

The presentation ceremony got under way and Jahangir was hailed again. He received a superb gold and silver trophy that was encrusted with diamonds. Rahmat watched it all with satisfaction but he was not carried away: 'Yes, Jahangir is getting better. Give me six months and he'll be better still. Ready for anything.' They were chilling words for Jansher who was left to reflect that he had never before played so well and lost so badly.

As soon as the formalities were over, Jahangir went to the Press Room to telephone his father in Pakistan. Roshan and the rest of the family were delirious with joy. Jahangir had proved that he was still the Conqueror of the World. In the context of his long succession of defeats, it was an astonishing comeback. Another tribute to patience, dedication and the restored partnership between player and coach.

What makes a world champion? Hanif Khan tells all his pupils at the PAF Centre in Peshawar that they will need five qualities to make it to the top: strength, stamina, style, sense, suppleness. Jahangir had them all in abundance. When his stamina became suspect, he fell from grace. When it was regained, he was in a league of his own. Rahmat adds three more qualities to the list: pride, being a Pathan, and professionalism. Pride in achievement burns inside Jahangir. His Pathan heritage dictates all he does. His complete professionalism is now a by-word in the sport.

Jahangir is honoured by his peers. They queue up with words of praise. Ross Norman: 'Best player of all time when he's playing well.' Hiddy Jahan: 'Miles better than anyone else in sight.' Phil Kenyon: 'Jahangir's the greatest player of the lot. I took on Hunt in his prime and he was more of a Jansher, wearing you down. Barrington never played often enough to give other players the chance to beat him. Jahangir takes us all on. He's up there on his own.' Chris Dittmar: 'I've played Jahangir and Jansher in World Open finals. Jansher is good. He'll beat me, maybe, but it'll take him the best part of two hours to do it. But Jahangir . . . he can *murder* you. I've played my balls off to beat him and never got near him. People talk about my racket-work and Rodney Martin's. But Jahangir can teach us all. He's so fast and brilliant. Only when you've played him can you appreciate just how good he is. He's far and away the best player for me.'

Those judgements were all given during the period when Jahangir was on a losing streak. His fellow-professionals still rated him as the finest player alive. On Friday, 13 May 1988, he fulfilled everything that was said about him. Jahangir would be the first to acknowledge Rahmat's vital contribution. The latter felt that he had failed as a player because he only reached twelfth position in the rankings. That was not good enough for a member of the dynasty. Like father, like son. It was as a coach that he was to explore the higher reaches of the game.

Amsterdam vindicated him as much as it did Jahangir. Much criticism had been aimed at Rahmat. It was said that he was unwise to expose Jahangir to a string of demoralising defeats. He should have been pulled out and trained up until he was ready for Jansher. Neither player nor coach saw it that way. They would hide from nobody. Jahangir therefore suffered repeated indignities in his search for victory over the new star. He finally achieved it.

Their future is rich with promise. A revitalised Jahangir will not rest until he has reconquered his empire and become the undisputed number one. Rahmat will be with him at every stage. But their efforts will not be exclusively devoted to Jahangir's playing career. Their horizons are much wider. Rahmat has coaching commitments with young players whom he is trying to bring on. He also has plans for team squash and for a series of challenge matches. Again, he and Jahangir are committed to a new charity organisation called Global Aid. This was the brainchild of Stuart Sharp who launched it with a pop record called 'Africa'. He wrote both the words and music of the song and has arranged for a percentage of the royalties to go towards Global Aid's first target – the building of a sports complex in an inner city area of a major provincial city. Jahangir and Rahmat Khan are endorsing the venture.

Early this year, the record was given a live performance by the group, Miracle, in the unlikely setting of Wembley Squash Centre. Jahangir and Umar Hayat Khan first hypnotised the audience with an exhibition match, then Sharp explained what Global Aid was about and how his record was the first tiny part of its contribution towards helping the underprivileged. Seated in the audience were members of Watford Football Club who were mesmerised by the sight of the Khans in action. Rahmat is now to be linked with the club, applying the training techniques he uses for squash and giving the soccer players a fresh approach. Elton John is thrilled with this initiative.

Apart from the round of tournaments and exhibition matches, there will be many such projects for the Khans in the future. They have reached the top of their profession but they have not lost sight of their humble origins. Providing sporting opportunities for everyone is now one of their major priorities. Stuart Sharp joined them as a film director all those years ago. Now he heads the charity organisation.

The Khans have one further ambition: to continue the dynasty that has written its name in letters a mile high across the sport. Amanat, son of Torsam, is currently spending six months in England as part of an assessment programme. He will devote himself to training. The young teenager's physical and mental capabilities are being put under the microscope. If he has the temperament and the talent, he will be groomed as the next in line. It is an unnerving thought for the rest of the squash world. When Jahangir retires, his successor may be standing in the wings. If not Amanat, it will be someone else from the family.

It was in 1951 that Hashim Khan introduced spectators to the qualities of his family. Those qualities have enriched squash ever since and they were on display in Amsterdam in 1988. Just when doubters were beginning to write the dynasty off, it came back with a champion. Jahangir Khan justified all those superlatives which have rained down on him over the years. He had been through a dark night of sorrow but had never lost faith. In every sense, the sun broke through in Holland.

There was an interesting footnote to the triumph. On the day after Jahangir won his sixth World Open title, Wimbledon beat the mighty Liverpool in the FA Cup at Wembley. Wimbledon. Torsam would have liked that. Wembley. That had significance for Rahmat and Jahangir.

It was quite a week for the Khan dynasty.

INDEX

Adarrago, Austin 165
Afghanistan 13
Afridis 14, 17, 26
Ahmed, Maqsood 96, 106, 126, 143, 144
Alauddin, Gogi 82, 86, 87, 90, 91, 92, 96, 97, 115–6, 121, 125, 145
Al Falaj 156, 160
Allah 24, 78–9, 113, 141, 142, 167
Amin, Ibraham 61, 71
Amin, Mohamed 49, 50
Artif, Brigadier 120
Asian Championship 138
Asran, Mo 139
Australia 80, 104, 109–12, 118, 137, 147
Australian Amateur Championship 74
Australian Open 85, 87, 114
Aziz, Ali 125, 148
Awad, Gamal 2, 126, 128, 129, 138, 139, 145, 147, 151–2

Baluchistan 12
Bangladesh 102
Barbizon Palace Hotel 164, 168
Barbour, Neven 114–5
Bari, Abdul 22, 35–6, 43, 44, 45, 52, 53, 63, 65
Barrington, Major Charles 66
Barrington, Jonah 4, 5, 64–71, 73–9, 82–5, 89–92, 97, 104, 108, 125, 131–2, 161
Barrington, Madeline 76–7, 131–2
Barrington, Nick 64, 67
Bath Club 60
Bavarian Open 145
Bellamy, Rex 74

Bey, Amr (Abdel Fattah Amr) 46, 61
Bhutto, Zulfiqar Ali 96, 102, 120
Biddle, Bert 52
Bombay 35, 41
Borg, Bjorn 3
Borrett, Norman 61
Briars, Gawain 125, 144
Brisbane Open 147
British Empire 12, 33, 39
British Open 1, 2, 5, 31–2, 43, 46, 53–5, 68–71, 77, 79, 82–3, 85, 90, 93, 134–6, 145, 152, 156, 159, 161–2
British Under-23 Open 109, 127–8
Broomfield, Nigel 61
Brownlee, Bruce 118, 126, 128
Bruce Court 60, 71
Brumby, Glen 109, 148
Butcher, Don 32

Calcutta Cricket Club 42
Canada 72, 104, 109, 118, 128, 138–42, 156
Caroe, Sir Olaf 13
Carter, Dick 74, 84
Chichester 89, 130, 133–5, 145, 151
Corby, Mike 69, 89

Davis, Steve 3
Dardir, Mohamed 80
de Mesquita, Norman 165
Dittmar, Chris 152, 157, 161, 164, 166–9, 172
Dittmar, Leanne 167
Donnelly, Frank 110
Dunlop Open 52, 54–5, 89, 159

Easter, John 92, 96
Eaton, Richard 128, 132

Edinburgh, Duke of 88–9
Edgbaston Priory 75, 77, 79, 118, 128
Egyptian Open 74
Engle, Brigadier 44

Fairburn, Alan 61
Fleet Club, Karachi 72, 98, 99, 146
French Open 152, 156, 160, 164
Frieling, Hans 165

Gandhi, Mohandas 33, 37
Gezira Sporting Club 46
Gilgit 136–7
Goldwyn, Sam 48
Global Aid 173
Gul brothers 95, 106
Gymkhana Club 49, 50, 95

Hamer, Malcolm 132
Hayman, Henry 51–2
Harris, Del 166
Harvard Club 57
Hidayatullah 149
Hildick-Smith, Gavin 61
Hill, Ricki 165
Hiscoe, Ken 74, 79, 84, 90–4, 96, 108
Horry, John 43, 44, 52, 53, 65
Hughes, Denis 68, 75
Hunt, Geoff 74, 78, 83–4, 90–2, 96–7, 105, 108, 118, 128–30, 133–41, 145, 152, 161
Husain, Mairaj 149
Hussain, Ghulam 86

Ibbotson, Derek 76
Ibbotson, Madeline 76–7, 131–2
India 6, 12, 32, 35, 37–9, 40, 43
Indian National Congress 32, 33, 37
Irish Open 125, 144
Islam 24–5, 137–8, 148
ISPA (International Squash Players Association) 108, 118, 125, 130, 144

Jahan, Hiddy 2, 81, 86–7, 90–2, 95, 109, 114–7, 121, 125, 134, 138–9, 143–5, 151, 158, 172
Jahan, Shah 95, 157
Jahan, Susan 116
Jaski, Adrian 128

Jawaid, Aftab 71, 73, 82
Jinnah, Mohamed Ali 37, 42
Junior Carlton Club 52, 53, 63, 64

Kaoud, Abbas 88
Karachi 39, 41, 49, 72–3, 119, 138, 142, 150, 160
Karim, el Mahmoud 44–6, 52, 61
Kelly, Commander 44
Kennedy, John F. 57
Kenyon, Phil 110–1, 138, 148, 152, 165, 172
Khan, Abdullah 18, 19–20
Khan, Abdul Ghaffar 26, 29, 39
Khan, Abdul Majeed 18, 20, 22, 26, 35
Khan, Aman 5, 49, 73–5, 77, 79, 80, 82, 93–5, 106, 116–7, 136
Khan, Amanat 173–4
Khan, Atlas 95, 96, 110–1
Khan, Azam 20, 21, 25, 26, 39–40, 42, 63, 68, 95, 101, 147
  childhood 27–8
  character 171
  achievements 5, 49–54, 57–9, 62, 97
Khan, Aziz 22, 72, 95
Khan, Faizullah 22–3, 26, 28, 30, 34, 40, 62, 100
Khan, Genghis 14
Khan, Gul Ahmed 95
Khan, Gulmast 72
Khan Hashim 20, 39–40, 42, 63, 72, 95–7, 101, 147, 152, 161–2
  childhood 18–20, 26–8, 97
  character 20–1, 25, 171, 174
  achievements 5–6, 35–6, 43–51, 53–4, 58–9, 61–2, 82, 97, 134, 143
Khan, Hassan 72, 99, 103, 107, 119, 126
Khan, Ismatullah 20–1
Khan, Jahangir 98 and onwards
  achievements ix–x, 106 and onwards. See also under specific achievements, e.g. British Open
  childhood 72, 95, 98–105
  character 103
Khan, Jansher 95, 149, 158–61, 164–6, 168–71
Khan, Josephine (Josie) 106, 122, 153
Khan, Liaqat 72

Khan, Mohibullah, senior 5, 53, 54, 57–9, 62, 63, 69, 72, 95, 96, 97, 101, 147, 171
Khan, Mohibullah, junior 86, 87, 91, 92, 96, 121, 126, 145, 149
Khan, Muhammed Ali 18, 21, 22
Khan, Mumtaz 86
Khan, Nasrullah 20, 36, 39, 40–1, 42, 74, 88, 93
  childhood 22–31, 34, 49, 50
  character 25, 75–9, 82–3, 85
  achievements 5, 6, 52, 55, 62–76, 94
  death, 104–5
Khan, Natasha 140
Khan, Nur 87, 95, 120, 121–2, 144
Khan, Rahmat 5, 7, 18, 49, 73–5, 90, 93, 95, 106, 108–9, 116–7, 119–27, 129–37, 139–41, 144, 146–7, 151, 153, 157, 159, 161–2, 166–73
  character 79–80, 82, 89
  achievements 5, 87, 92, 94, 104
Khan, Roshan 7, 40, 42, 63, 67, 95, 98–105, 117, 119, 120–1, 126, 135, 138, 144, 147, 150, 151, 171
  childhood 22–6, 28–31, 34, 39
  character 25, 81, 105, 111–12, 143, 171
  achievements 5, 43, 48–59, 61, 62, 72–3, 97
Khan, Safirullah 20, 49, 86, 95
Khan, Said Ali 21–2
Khan, Sharif 5, 62, 72, 95
Khan, Torsam 7, 49, 63, 72, 95, 99–101, 106–10, 113–4, 122–4
  character 80–2, 91, 93–4, 145–6
  achievements 87–92, 103–4
  death 5, 114–9, 140, 142
Khan, Umar Daraz 86
Khan, Umar Hayat 166, 173
Khan, Zahir 107, 128
Kvant, Lars 110

Lahore 29, 86
Lansdowne Club 46, 52, 60–1, 76, 79, 85
Lee, Danny 128
Lyon, Jeremy 69, 82

Mahsuds 17
Malaysian Open 152

Marciano, Rocky 3
Martin, Rodney 159, 161–2, 164, 166
McKay, Heather 3
Mennen Cup 152
Miles, Eustace 11
Mocatta, John 64–5
Molaviya, Mohen Madan Pandit 32
Mohmunds 26, 27
Monaco Open 161, 168
Moses, Ed 3
Muhammed, Meer 73
Mulcaster, Richard 9
Muneer, Sajjad 87, 92
Muslims 5, 12, 24, 38, 40, 120–1
Muslim League 33, 37–8

Nancarrow, Cam 74, 90–2
Navratilova, Martina 3
Nawakille 17–26, 29, 35, 47, 62, 150
Nehru, Jawaharlal 37, 39–40
Newbolt, Sir Henry 11
New Grampians Club 57, 68
Nicklaus, Jack 3
Norman, Ross 126, 128, 145, 155–60, 166, 168–9, 172
North-West Frontier 5, 12, 28–9, 39

Owens, Jesse 3

PAF Officers Club 87, 105, 171
Pakistan 6, 7, 38, 43, 51, 101–3, 109, 143
Pakistan Navy 50, 51, 57, 150
Pakistan Open 150–1, 159
Palmer, Mike 93
Paris 145, 160
Parsee Cricket Club of Bombay 42
Partition 22, 38–42
Pathans 5, 6, 12–14, 17, 22, 23, 25–9, 39, 55, 60, 66, 70, 86, 112, 149–51, 172
Patrick International Festival 2, 130, 145, 151
Patterson, Brian 139
Peshawar 14, 25, 40, 47, 86, 149, 171
Peshawar Club 15–16, 18, 20–3, 26–9
PIA (Pakistan International Airlines) 94–7, 101, 106, 120, 126, 150, 160

Qaiser, Sohail 134
Quraishi, A. J. 101

Rahman, Mujibur 102
Rai-Amstelhal 164, 168
Ranjitsinhji, Prince 42
Rawalpindi 29–30, 40
Rawalpindi Club 18, 28, 30–1
Raza, Group-Captain 45
Redshirts 26, 27, 29
Reedman, Bill 92
Reid, C. R. 31, 32
Richards, Gordon 3
Robertson, Chris 165
Robinson, John 157

Saddar 14–15
Safwat, Achmed 89, 90, 92, 152
Sahib, Dr. Khan 26, 29
Saleem, Mohamed 96, 106, 145
Sanchez, Mario 147
Shafik, Tewfik 68
Sharp, Stuart 132–3, 136–9, 144–5, 173
Sherren, Mike 134
Sind Club 49, 95
South African Amateur Championship 74
Spanish Open 156, 158, 160
Swiss Masters 144, 148, 156
Swiss Open 159–60

Talbott, Mark 147, 152
Taleb, Abou (Abdelfattah Ahmed Aboutaleb) 57 ,68–71, 80
Thurger, Mike 88

US Open 1, 62, 72, 156, 159–60
Unsquashable 107, 109, 110, 146, 153

Victorian Championship 84
Victorian Junior Championship 84

Wadey, Joyce 107
Watson, Roland 92, 144
Waziris 17
Waziristan 32
Wembly Squash Centre 38, 107, 108, 132, 173
Welsh Open 88, 138
Wilkie, Don 170
Williams, Dean 134, 139, 147, 148
Willstrop, Christy 128
Wilson, Roy 61
Wimbledon Squash and Badminton Club 79
World Amateur Championship 1, 74, 109
World Masters 138, 147, 152
World Open Championship 1, 2, 93, 126, 138–42, 147–8, 152, 156–9, 164–72
World Team Championship 74, 94–7, 156
Wucha Jawar 27

Yasin, Mohamed 79, 82–3, 91, 92, 94, 145, 159, 168, 169
Yusufzais 17

Zaman, Qamar 86, 87, 90–2, 95–7, 121, 126, 134, 138, 145, 148, 152
Zia-al-Haq, President 120